Showdown Semester:
Advice from a Writing Professor

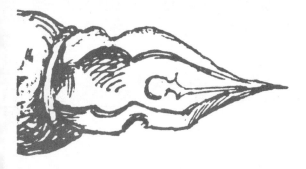

Martin Russ

CROWN PUBLISHERS, INC.   NEW YORK

Library of Congress Cataloging in Publication Data

Russ, Martin.
  Showdown semester.

  1. College teaching. I. Title.
LB2331.R8   1980   378'.125   80-20335
ISBN: 0-517-542137
Design by Camilla Filancia
10 9 8 7 6 5 4 3 2 1
First Edition

for Cara,
friend of the family

Showdown Semester

Wednesday, September 6, 1978

Flattered by your request, Curly—but unsure what sort of stuff you want me to write down. I'm teaching one fiction and one nonfiction course this semester. Will you be teaching nonfiction too? I'll assume that the answer's yes, and will try to keep you posted on both courses. Here goes:

FIRST CLASS, EXPOSITION I (meets Monday, Wednesday, Friday, 12:30–1:20) Usually I start off by explaining and assigning the five-minute speeches, but today I decided to wait until next week—"after things have settled down and some of you have taken the opportunity to flee in terror." The students chuckled nervously, for I had just devoted ten minutes trying to convince the weak-hearted to drop the course. "*Heavy* work load," I told them. "*Many* writing assignments." I warned them that they're the ones who will will be doing all the work, while the instructor sits back and makes rotten remarks about it.

—Keep a straight face in class. Never laugh or even smile at your own humorously intended remarks. Better to pretend that you are unaware of being funny. It's all right to smile when a student is funny, though—but make it a wan smile. Avoid undue joviality. Never be genial. Avoid nice-guyism. A slight suggestion of menace is helpful. I manage that by merely sitting quietly behind my face. You

1

with your kindly puss probably won't be able to pull it off. Just don't be too nice. Otherwise the students will attack at once.

—Read aloud the names on the class list, asking the students to correct your pronunciation. Get each to tell you what his major course of study is—and anything else you can get him to say. This is the first step in forcing the students out of the anonymity they all prefer.

—Have something to suck on in class; you'll need it from time to time. I smoke an occasional cigarette while teaching, but judging from the way this Vote Yes on Proposition No is going I won't be able to get away with it much longer. Over the past six years certain students have scribbled "Quit Smoking" in answer to "What might the teacher do to improve his teaching?" on the teacher/course evaluation form. I've tried chewing gum, but it causes you to mumble in a disgustingly juicy manner. A small thermos bottle filled with something is probably the best solution.

—Talk beforehand to the department secretary or if necessary the chairman about where your classes will be held. Make sure you aren't stuck in a seminar room where everyone sits around a table rubbing elbows and knees and the students can peek at your notes. Never let anyone see your notes; otherwise, grotty rumors will start bouncing around the corridors.

I've been assigned to Porter Hall 125C for the Expo course; it's spacious enough that the students are set back from the instructor. (Everyone over twelve looks a lot better anyway from a distance.) Porter Hall 125C is good too because there's no direct sunlight—unlike the rooms across the hall, where you have to squint on sunny mornings and your pants get stuck to the chair on warm afternoons. (Everyone over twelve looks a lot better in the shade anyway, don't you find?)

—These are probably not the kind of notes you had in mind.

FIRST CLASS, FICTION WORKSHOP (meets Monday and Wednesday, 2:30–4:20) You can get closer to your fiction-workshop students than to those in nonfiction; that's because the former are forced to do more talking and reveal themselves through their writing in a way that is unnecessary in nonfiction. One can write a shelf-full of nonfiction books without revealing much about oneself; with fiction it's a different story.

—Think about roughening yourself up a little, Curly, before you meet your first class. Nothing gets a student's back up in quite the same way as an instructor who is too squared away—the male who is too tailored, pipe at perfect angle, tattersall vest just so, or the female clotheshorse with matching this and color-coordinated that. When I started to work here six years ago there was a certain instructor the students made fun of (behind his back, of course); later I found out it was largely because he was so splendidly turned out.

In a way you have to be an actor in the classroom, or at least a performer, and your costume is more important than you may realize. I wouldn't dream of making specific suggestions to a woman in this matter, but as a general rule I would avoid pretending to be unpretentious.

—The instructor needs to spend a certain amount of time reminding students indirectly that he's human, which some find hard to accept.

3

—Take attendance. Hardly any instructors do so nowadays, and students skip classes freely. This is demoralizing not only to the instructor but also to the students. I recommend that you warn them fiercely at the first meeting that a perfect attendance record is a requirement. I tell them I'm unforgiving in this matter, that my ego is so swollen with self-importance that when I spy an empty chair I consider it a personal insult, that when someone skips a class I find it impossible from that point on to take him seriously as a student. They always chuckle when I say this, but a few of them wonder if I mean it.

If you fail to give them a dire warning of *some* kind, there will be several absences in every class; those students who miss homework assignments, in-class exercises, and lectures are likely to buttonhole you in the hallway later, demanding to know what they've missed. You'll be expected to stand there and in sixty seconds or so deliver a lecture that took you an hour that morning. Sometimes it's hard to avoid kicking the person before you in the shins at such moments, and so it's best to take strong preemptive measures early on.

You might also mention in the first class that when you fill out the student evaluation form at the end of the semester you will include their attendance record, and that a perfect record makes a favorable impression on most prospective employers.

"A poor attendance record will result in a poor grade," I tell them. "That may strike you as grossly unfair, but this is not a democratically run shop."

Friday, September 8

—Memorize their names quickly. The best way is to write down a brief word caricature as you take attendance in the opening class: sensational blonde, surly freak, etc. (Be careful students don't see this when they come up to chat with you after the bell.)

Later, when the students turn in their first assignment, take note of the way they sign their names. If Charles Miller signs himself Chuck Miller you can call him Chuck in class—and you should; but if he writes Charles call him Charles. Never ask what they prefer to be called; it smacks of good-guyism.

—Get the students talking! The biggest problem in the second class, you'll find, is to get them to say anything; and if you can't, they'll tend to remain silent throughout the remaining forty-two meetings and you'll have nightmares and go crazy before Christmas.

Here's an all-purpose question to ask whenever you don't know what else to do: "Any questions?"

And here's what to say when someone asks a question you can't answer: "That's a very good question. Does anyone else have a very good question?"

And, finally, here's what you can say in moments of panic: "That's a very good question. Don't ask it again."

A peculiar and not at all trivial problem at this stage is that the students are so shy you can barely hear what they're saying, especially if the air-conditioner is on. Avoid

5

snapping at them in an authoritarian manner ("Speak up!"). They are so tense it's best to ask them in an almost ludicrously gentle way to speak louder: "Would you ask that again, please? Sounds like an important question." If you still can't hear what they're saying, approach the student with your hand cocked behind your ear.

EXPOSITION 1 The main body of the class was devoted to explaining the requirements for the five-minute speech they'll all have to give, with particular attention to the Specific Purpose Statement at the beginning. I've found the SPS to be a very effective teaching device. The principle is simple: Writing an SPS before you do anything else forces you to figure out exactly what you're going to say. If you know what you want to say, then you can say it; if you don't, you can't.

The requirements for the speech: five minutes long. Don't read it. You can refer to notes on one side of an index card. The speech must be aimed at a general audience. You must interpret the material in some way, i.e., convey an attitude toward your topic rather than merely pass along a series of facts. Don't tell us what we already know. The speech shouldn't personally embarrass anyone in the room.

Suggested structure:
1. Tell us what you're *going* to tell us (that's the SPS).
2. *Tell* us (that's the main body).
3. Tell us what you've just *told* us (that's the recapitulation).

Several years ago a student gave a speech about what a lousy course this was, and a couple of weeks later another described—in scary detail, and convincingly—how and why he was going to commit suicide. It happened that both students fulfilled the requirements and so got an enthusiastic thumbs-up from me, much to their surprise; but the following semester I added the requirement about the speech not being embarrassing to anyone in the room. The first student, incidentally, dropped the course soon after and the second works for U.S. Steel.

Monday, September 11

FICTION WORKSHOP I recommend that you read each story at least three times. During the opening discussion you'll impress the students by being more familiar with the work than the writer himself, and your minutely detailed remarks will set the standard for close and careful reading henceforth. Try to arrange it so that the first two or three stories you choose are by the most talented students, so that you can do more praising than fault-finding. Ripping the first story apart would stun the students into permanent numbness and you'd get little out of them for the rest of the semester. Try to start off as sweetly as possible; they discover soon enough what a rotter you are.

—Too many teachers respond to student papers by scratching a general comment at the top and a handful of trivial comments in the margin, and if there's one thing that bothers writing students more than anything else it's insufficient feedback. I recommend that you correct everything it's possible to correct—or rather that you indicate every area where an improvement can be made. (Let the student himself do the improving; never do his work for him.) This often means that you'll take issue with literally every sentence. So be it; if it can be improved, it should be.

—Undergrads tend to write clever-tricky stories devoid of emotion. Tell them to cut it the hell out. (You have to be a perfect churl at times.)

—When you open the discussion for the first time, let them do most of the talking. They'll have a lot to say about the story; let 'em say it. This will set the pattern, and you'll be able to do more listening than talking throughout the course. One earns one's pay by responding to their comments; they'll tell you, indirectly, what they need to know. The worst thing you can do is establish a pattern of domination by yammering away throughout the first two or three class periods. If you do that, you'll find that the students have nothing at all to say when you ask for comments: you will have intimidated them into silence, and if you've ever tried to deliver twenty-eight consecutive two-hour lectures on The Art of Fiction you know what purgatory is.

—Another way to loosen them up at the start is to give out the following assignment: "Bring in a written statement of your fiction aesthetic next time, an artistic manifesto." Undergrads always respond enthusiastically, handing in page after page of grand, sweeping, vacuous assertions, which I carefully file away without reading. Monci Jo Nickerson, an artsy-craftsy junior of the waif variety (long straight hair nearly obscuring her lovely plain face), wandered up after class to say she was "extremely turned on" at being given the opportunity at last to declare herself artistically. If I wanted to be nasty, which I do, I could point out that most students are far more comfortable talking about The Art of Fiction than doing it.

—It would probably be a mistake to engage in sexual innuendo with your undergrads, even though you'll be much closer to them in age than I am. Nothing to do with prudishness; it's simply that most undergrads are excruciatingly self-conscious and unsure of themselves on the mating front, and sexually oriented wordplay makes them nervous as hell—although most of them would die before admitting it.

If your attitudes about love are reactionary (they'll probably be considered so by your students, since you're over thirty), for God's sake don't let them know it. The student story I just finished reading is among other things an expression of contempt for marital fidelity. That their instructor has been faithfully married to the same woman for seventeen years is something that best go undiscovered; I wouldn't enjoy being pitied by undergraduates.

You will find a strong element of nervous giggling behind the façade of sexual sophistication, and instructors of an older generation who are themselves perhaps a little nervous about the whole matter need to prepare themselves for two things: (1) being shocked at the loveless sexual encounters described in student stories (not so much the encounters themselves as the passionless, clinical, anti-pornographic point of view) and (2) the raucous laughter that breaks out whenever you make a sexually oriented remark, intentionally or not. Last week I was talking about a certain method of storytelling and at one point said, "It depends on how you do it. Do you do it well? If so, then do it a lot. But if—" At their unexpected snickering I looked up and found them leering like fourth graders whose teacher had said something about Balaam's ass.

—While I'm in an irascible mood: You'll have to accommodate yourself somehow to the pseudocelebration of the grotesque so often found in undergrad fiction—great sweeping hunks of despair, futility, greed, sadism, nihilism, cynicism, anarchism. I don't think for a moment that undergrads are sincerely concerned about such concepts; it's only that all this is currently chic, and sophomores are burdened with the belief that these are the very things a writer should write about. Honest feeling is pretty rare in undergrad fiction at the beginning of the semester, and you can perform a useful service by helping them get in touch with their gizzards. If you have the nerve (which I don't), you might even try convincing them there's a difference between right and wrong, good and bad. Since they belong to the everything's-relative generation you'll probably be wasting your time, though.

Friday, September 15

Unless you're an unusually charming teacher with a talent for reassurance, you'll find the students very tense during the first two weeks of the semester. Tension and resentment are natural partners, and you'll probably have to deal with some open resentment at the beginning. This

10

often manifests itself in the form of total student opposition to anything you have to say. There are times when a class is so high-strung that you can comment mildly on the weather outside and someone will demand that you justify the educational value of your observation. "None whatever," you respond cheerily. The trick is to get them talking, and let them talk as much as they need to up to the point of raving or incoherent rambling; that'll get rid of some of the pressure. There's something very comforting, and surprising, about being listened to, especially if you're an undergrad and the listener is a professor. Keep in mind that very few of your colleagues actually listen carefully to their students; more often than not they lend an ear in a sort of auto-pilot manner as if they already know what the student is going to say.

If a student begins to ramble, you can choke him off gently with, "And so your point is . . . ?"

Listening intensely is more than a disarming device; it strongly encourages the student to think before he speaks in class, and maybe even outside of class.

Work in as many indirect compliments as you can without being obsequious, not to mention insincere. Always be sincere, even when you don't mean it. "That's interesting," you can say at the end of a comment, or "That's quite true," or "Yes, that carries the idea a step further." Answer respectfully even if the remark is stupid and the others are howling derisively. Don't ever say "You're wrong" or "I disagree" or "You've missed the point, ace." Answer in a positive and courteous manner: "You're halfway there. Let's see who can take it a step further." If the comment is irredeemably moronic you can always say "That's an unusual point of view."

11

—Always stop dead at the bell. Students go deaf as soon as it rings and begin gathering up their books and papers, pulling on their coats, thinking about the upcoming class and whether they have time to grab a cup of coffee on the way. Make sure, therefore, to give the upcoming assignment well before the bell rings.

—If you make a faux pas or blunder in class or if anything happens that makes you feel the fool, don't brood over it. There's no need; the students will have forgotten it by the beginning of the next class. Their wretched lives are so fragmented, their attention yanked in so many directions every day, that the only time they'll think about you—and then only incidentally—is when they're seated in your classroom.

—If you happen to know already what your weakness as a teacher is going to be, it's a smart idea to tip them off to it beforehand. If, for instance, your weakness is disorganization, you can slip in a remark such as this: "Organization is not exactly my strong suit, you understand." Undergrads tend to be contemptuous of poorly organized teachers—unless they happen to be charmingly disorganized like my colleague in the modern languages department, Yves Mirandelle, who begins each class muttering crankily to himself as he piles the desk high with textbooks and research papers and then seems to spend the rest of the hour crawling around after whatever has fallen to the floor, and incidentally never referring to any of it during class.

—It may gall you to hear this, but undergrads expect to be entertained as well as educated. While it may not be necessary to do a striptease every Friday, it is necessary to bring in challengingly interesting material, and you can slyly snake in your dry but essential "educational stuff" along the way.

—Always be ready to answer the following appropriate and sensible but otherwise unsettling question: "What's the point of this?" Getting your students to ask "What's the point of this?" should be one of your major goals as a writing teacher, even though you're only going to be teaching for the one semester.

—Don't be too complimentary to the one student who is unusually intelligent and articulate and/or talented. There's always one such stand-out, usually a girl. In the Expo class it's Melissa Harkness, who for indefinable reasons makes me think of Radcliffe in the Fifties whenever I look at her; in the Fiction Workshop it's Abigail Boretsky, a tall, black-haired girl with piercing gypsy eyes. If you acknowledge the relative brilliance of such students in any way, their classmates will begin to think of them as teacher's pets and cat claws will be unsheathed. Be even-handed in your compliments.

—Occasionally you'll have to deal with aggressively hostile undergrads—The Stridents, I call them. You can't always tell who will turn out to be a Strident: it's rarely the sullen fellow in the back row or the bitch goddess up front; more likely it'll turn out to be the bland-faced kid somewhere in the middle. When he reveals himself (he'll suddenly want to engage you in a heated argument), simply answer his objection with literal-minded logic, turning it into a principle or concept to be examined as an intellectual exercise by the class as a whole. If you play dumb, so to speak, giving the impression that it's inconceivable that a student should try to provoke you, soon it will be inconceivable to the student himself. As I believe in passive sadism in childrearing, so I advocate the same stance in dealing with the obstreperous strident. Kill him with kindness or at least benevolent inattention. Not only must you never let yourself be drawn into any sort of emotional escalation, you must even avoid acknowledging his attitude. Nonacknowledgment is the purest of punishments. I have no particular student in mind, by the way; everyone has been really quite ruly up to now, but my four-year-old Molly is presently crying and hurling pillows around in the next room, obliterating the universe symbolically, and all she needs is a nap, not a lecture. I'm sitting here ignoring her.

Monday, September 18

FICTION WORKSHOP I gave them an assignment to be turned in on Monday: three to five pages of dialogue in which two people surprise each other with revelations of character.

I read aloud from *Smiles of a Summer Night* (the scene in which Lawyer Eggerman visits his former mistress at home, her husband then returning unexpectedly) as an example of the orchestration of characters revealing themselves in a tense situation; and then another from *The Seventh Seal* (the beginning of the chess game between the Knight and Death) as an example of "intellectual conversation" that's dramatically interesting. This latter was in response to a class discussion last week about a student story that was little more than an undramatic academic collo-quy. The students were reluctant to believe that an intellectual conversation devoid of emotion tends to be dull in a novel or play or story. Nor were they ready to hear that in fiction the writer should stick with the emotional over the intellectual as much as possible. Often the two can go together, of course, as in a heated dialectical discussion—as long as one or both of the characters have something personally at stake.

Terence O'Haggarty (son and grandson and brother of doctors, determined to become a nondoctor novelist) asked today if it's necessary to be a dutiful reader. He wanted to know if one has to lean over backward for every Author, if one has to dig hard for meanings and stay on the alert for second and third levels and study mythology to understand the parallels and allusions and so on. It was a wonderful question, but in a way I wish he hadn't asked it. My response turned out to be indigestible: "We have no duties as readers. We aren't even duty-bound to finish reading the story or novel. It is the *writer* who has the duty—to entertain and move us. I have spoken."

The students were appalled, not having yet learned that one doesn't need to finish *Portrait of the Artist as a Young Man* if one happens to find it boring. English majors have an almost religious awe of Literature and it's always getting in their way. The notion that a work of art is meant to be enjoyed—to use and throw away and maybe reuse later if you feel like it—is considered almost blas-phemous. Bud Carr in his yellow "Cat" cap and tiny Van-dyke stared at me in stunned disbelief and said that he couldn't disagree more.

"Life is short," I explained.

Ira Rosenberg wanted to know if my attitude toward "the classics" wasn't dangerous. I don't know whether he meant dangerous to my reputation or what, but I explained that at forty-seven, while I sincerely wish I had time to read the entire works of Honoré de Balzac in French I planned on being a corpse within thirty years.

—Occasionally you'll need to patronize a student or say something condescending. You can get away with it by tipping him off beforehand: "I know this is condescending (or patronizing) but—."

EXPOSITION I In your nonfiction-writing class always be ready to "tie in" whatever you're talking about with its application out in the world. Undergrads are terribly conscious that they'll soon become human beings, and are delighted to know that some of the stuff they're learning may be useful after they leave this artificial hothouse called college. As a writing teacher you'll have more of an advantage in this regard than teachers of most of the other "humanities" courses.

Wednesday, September 20

Along about the third week your students are going to realize that nearly everything you have to say about their work is negative—despite the fogbank of weasel words that I recommend you use—and you'll find the class as a whole turning hostile. No one enjoys being criticized, and there's no way of making anyone hate it less. I try every semester, though. Here's one way that may work for you.

—When you hand back their corrected first assignments, open for discussion the issue of whether positive or negative criticism is more helpful in a practical way. I believe absolutely that a developing writer needs to hear more about what's wrong than about what's right, even though emotionally all anyone wants is praise and encouragement; but of course you don't put it that way in class. By the end of the discussion many of them will have convinced themselves that negative criticism is more helpful, and you can agree with them in a general way. Ask them then, as sweetly as possible, to accept therefore the rotten remarks you've slashed in red up and down the margins and between the lines not as negative criticism but as tentative suggestions toward improving their work. Then hand the papers back.

"The writer has a duty to make his writing as good as it can be made," you can tell them. "That's what professionalism is all about."

Some of them will like the ring of this and will be flattered to have been consulted in the matter; but when they look over your slashings they'll turn angry in an instant. Don't tease them about the apparent contradiction; don't even acknowledge it; just keep plugging along in a calm, dogged sort of way, showing them little ways to render their superb writing even more superb.

FICTION WORKSHOP We've taken a hard look at seven student stories so far, and all seven writers are to one degree or another disturbed and confused over our comments. Ira Rosenberg is openly disgusted. It seems that everyone in the workshop, including me, has something different to say about each story. Which comments should the writer accept, which reject? I tell them that their Unconscious will sort it all out effortlessly, absorbing what's useful, rejecting the rest. "Most of what you hear in the workshop is useless," I told them. "You needn't waste your time trying to figure out what's correct and what's incorrect. There's no correct/incorrect in this kind of criticism anyway; there's only useful and useless, and the unconscious part of your mind is the best judge."

—Among other things, you have to teach them how to take criticism. It can be done only indirectly; you'll get nowhere if you look a student in the eye and tell him to stop sulking and start listening. This pain quotient is something you have to keep very much in mind throughout the course. Even the most emotionally mature student will bridle whenever you speak negatively about his writing, no matter how positively you couch the remark. And you *should* couch everything positively, even your most negative comment—going to ludicrous extremes if necessary ("I'm crazy about the inventiveness in this section, but I can't help wondering if your distinctive style isn't a touch too subtle for some of your readers.").

The brute fact is, the instructor in a fiction workshop earns his pay by telling students what's wrong with their stories. The students themselves are convinced they need encouragement more than anything, and of course you'll encourage them as much as you can; but what they need most of all is discouragement, so that they'll come to realize how appallingly low their standards are and break the terrible habits they've learned. (The habit of writing fiction sloppily, for example. Many workshop students write articles for the *Tartan*, and invariably the composition is more precise than their one-draft fiction writings.)

Remember that an undergrad can swallow a negative comment much more readily if it comes from his peers. For it to hit home, and stick, all you need do is gently support it. "Does anyone have a comment on the theme of this story?" you might ask if a certain story happens to be pointless or is written in so opaque a style that the point is indiscernible; the students will do the rest.

Try using the Pauline method: Tell the sinner how wonderful he is before hitting him upside the head for worshipping idols.

By the way, it's not necessary for an undergrad to pay a hell of a lot of attention to what the other students are saying in a workshop, nor even to what the instructor is saying; in fact, too deliberate a concentration tends to obscure the pure work of the unconscious. It isn't a bad idea to warn your students that much of what they'll hear in the classroom is useless to them, and that when the semester's over they probably won't be able to state precisely what it is they've learned.

Try to explain this to the dean or the chairman or the literature or rhetoric professors and see how far you get, though. You may actually be forced to cough up a rationale from time to time. (Rationale: multipurpose academic word that can mean the thinking behind, the purpose, the goal, the method; sometimes it can even mean the reason.)

Last year there was a certain flurry of wattle-quivering among the tenured members of the department when it was discovered that none of the fiction workshops was "structured in a sequential manner." I whipped off a memo, had it copied and distributed, intending it as a sort of preemptive strike against a request for a rationale.

The teaching of creative writing, and the learning, is a nonlinear proposition. Although fiction workshops are occasionally labeled sequentially, this is hardly ever a matter of Beginning and Advanced but rather of Less Experienced and Experienced. Nor is it a matter of Hard, Harder, Hardest—nor even of Good, Better, Best—since one is dealing with creative work, and in a noncompetitive way. Nor is it a matter of acquiring knowledge from the outside, as in most courses of study. It is rather a matter of coming to understand, of learning how to control that which is already present within the student. No workshop student starts out with a little knowledge and ends up with a lot. It is a matter of uncovering bit by bit the given talent, and at the same time helping to control and exercise it in the most efficient and effective manner. Whatever talent or ability or potential thereof which the student brings to the workshop cannot be augmented by the instructor, any more than a coach can augment the talent of a young baseball player. Unlike most other courses of study available throughout the University, the student in the Creative Writing Program brings in his own ideas. He is asked not merely to define and analyze but also to conceive, create, shape, develop and polish. From the student's point of view, what happens is that he repeatedly encounters instructors who seek to convince him of the importance of characterization and interpretation, of plot, theme, setting and style; of the power of words, images, symbols; of the concepts of eloquence, overtone, wit and common-sense logic; of the importance of telling an interesting story about interesting people interestingly; and finally of the importance of rewriting and polishing. While there may be only one way, basically, to run a program through a computer, one way to speak French, one way to build a warehouse, one way to remove an appendix—the ways of telling a story are infinite, and the student, finally, has to settle on his own way. The process of helping him toward that goal cannot be structured programmatically, since it is a multidimensional, spontaneous, creative affair.

There was no response to this, neither from the chairman nor from a single colleague except Al Goldman, an advertising executive (from the "real world," note) who was teaching a course that semester. Which wasn't surprising, since the noble Catatonians are even more reluctant than sophomores to commit themselves to much of anything. The preemptive memo *may* have contributed to the absence of further interdepartmental fretting about the sequential structuring of workshops. Notice that in the memo some rather grandiose claims are made, but no indication of the methods by which *I* teach.

EXPOSITION I The second assignment was to write an angry letter to the *Tartan* (the campus newspaper, and a good one). After collecting them I told the class not to expect them back until Monday. (Our next class is on Friday.) Most teachers try to get papers back to students at the following meeting, but by returning them on Monday instead of Friday I can read three a day instead of six, can read them more carefully and interestedly, and spend more effort on editorial suggestions. In seven years of teaching not one student has complained about the delay, but I always explain it beforehand—otherwise students bug me about when they're going to get their papers back.

—Use the conditional tense liberally, even though you are demanding straight-ahead sentences from them: *Couldn't it be possible that . . . ? I wouldn't be surprised if . . . Should we overlook the fact that . . . ?* Students prefer to have a general goal pointed out and to be allowed to make the specific discovery themselves. I recommend that you use the word seems a lot, italicized, when you write comments on their papers. "This *seems* illogical"; "That *seems* an overstatement"; "I wonder if this wouldn't *seem* simplistic to some readers."

Bear in mind that undergrads, particularly freshmen and sophomores, are often more emotional than reasonable. Professor Florian Beeler admitted to me once that he devotes the first half of the semester to "wooing the undergrads" in his writing courses. This wooing business is exasperating sometimes. You want to march into the classroom, present your fifty minutes of material, march out. That's the way it's done in many of the best adult-education courses, and it's certainly the way I would want to learn something. Try this "march" stuff with undergrads and you'll lose your credibility in short order. I saw it happen when I was on the staff in the drama department. The instructor in question knew exactly what he wanted to do and say in every class (and as I shared several classes with him I can say that his material was excellent); but he made a fundamental mistake: he told the undergrads what they needed to know, and they, being half-adolescent still, resisted the material because they resisted him.

Let the students teach themselves as much as possible. Being taught something by someone else doesn't give one a sense of accomplishment—not if one is nineteen or twenty.

—Another reason for scribbling as many detailed comments on their work as possible: While on the one hand the student is mad at you for being so critical, on the other hand he's amazed and delighted that you've taken his work so seriously. I think the main reason freshman and sophomore writing is so lousy is that no one has ever carefully read anything these students have written since the day they first learned to write. Unfortunately, very few college teachers read undergrad papers carefully either, as you doubtless know.

—It's profitable to convince your students as soon as possible that there's such a thing as a worthless piece of writing. In grade school and high school and even in college they've all spent hours churning out worthless pieces of writing on demand, and it'll come as a shocking and perhaps delightful surprise to hear someone acknowledge this out loud. You needn't say that anything they've turned in to you is worthless; once they've grasped the concept itself they'll try not to turn in anything worthless from then on.

—Although you owe some office time to each student, you'll find that most visitors want to stick around too long and you need to know how to get rid of them without being rude. I've found the old-fashioned white lie most useful. "Oh-oh, it's almost three and I've got a meeting in Porter Hall." Usually the student will continue talking, and you'll have to stand up all agitated and begin stuffing papers into your briefcase. Occasionally the student will follow you down the hall, still talking, and you'll be forced to find an actual meeting to attend. If there are no meetings going on you'll have to leave the building with a purposeful air. Why not simply duck into the nearest toilet, you ask? Because some students are not at all shy about following you even there, and it's not easy to pee with a sophomore discussing the meaning of meaning at the adjoining urinal. Or in your case the adjoining stall.

—Do not hang around the hallways between classes. Students catching sight of you may decide on the spur of the moment that they absolutely must discuss Milton with you for three hours. I used to get ambushed frequently until I learned how to slither and slink on the back stairs, how to avoid saying hello to the stray student by pretending to be absorbed in a departmental memo. If you move briskly, frowning with surly concentration over the paper, no one will dare interrupt you. If you're caught without a memo and sense that someone is about to pounce, the only thing you can do is duck into the nearest toilet and take your chances. If a student traps you and you simply must get away, here's how to do it: Make an appointment for the following day, and nine times out of ten the student will forget to show up. If he does show up, here's a sure-fire method for limiting the conference to fifteen minutes—but it takes a little preparation. If the appointment is for 1:00 P.M., say, arrange to have a friend call you at 1:15. When the phone rings, pick it up, say hello, listen as if in growing dismay, mutter "I'll be right over," hang up, apologize all flustered to the student, usher him out, grab your briefcase, and follow him into the hall, pausing only long enough to lock your door. Students are rarely so aggressive as to insist on accompanying you to the emergency ward where your grandmother is having her head sewn back on.

Friday, September 22

The students will be impressed with your detailed comments, yes, but won't necessarily learn a hell of a lot from them. The only thing you can accomplish during your semester will be to teach them a few basic principles, and you have to be pretty heavy-handed about it. Better to cover too little ground heavy-handedly than too much ground delicately, subtly, wittily, brilliantly. Better that they end the semester with a handful of basic principles stuffed into their brains forever than a whole stewpan of doodlebug stuff that'll leak out before the end of Christmas vacation.

The most important principle is so simple as to be almost incomprehensible: *Make sure you have something to say before you write it down.* One of the most difficult things undergrads have to learn is that they have as yet little to say. It's a valuable and humbling discovery, but once a student learns it it's almost impossible for him to write anything pointless. (As to how you respond when a fiction student cries, "But that's the very point—the pointlessness!" I leave you to figure out for yourself.)

May I say once more that if you tip them off early on that you'll be employing certain distasteful teaching techniques (grinding repetition, for instance—my personal favorite) they'll give you lots of leeway to be insufferable. They'll also assume that the course is going to be as boring and burdensome and useless as most of their other courses and you'll be able to surprise them and send them on their way rejoicing.

FICTION WORKSHOP Many students have trouble understanding how important it is to dramatize as much of their material as possible; they'd much rather tell the reader about what happened than show it. I've never understood why this is so; perhaps it's only that they resist the notion of "being dramatic" and therefore corny.

25

Jennifer Balle's story yesterday was about a blind woman who had managed to convince her blind husband that she had always been partially sighted. Not a bad gimmick, actually, but Jennifer presented the whole thing expositionally, in a kind of summary form. *The funeral director told George that Mrs. Capotti had had two glass eyes all along.* This was the last line of the story and was meant to be a kind of O. Henry ending. I applauded her desire to try to surprise the reader but suggested that it would be more effective to fashion a series of *scenes* out of her material—showing the woman pretending to see in various situations, for instance. I had the students write a few lines of dialogue, turning the expositional sentence above into a short scene. Here's the most successful, by Abigail Boretsky:

George sensed that Mr. Benson had something important to tell him, but was too embarrassed to come right out with it.

"Something troubling you?" he asked.

Mr. Benson hemmed and then hawed. "Mrs. Scarpotti was blind, you know," he finally said.

"Of course."

"In both eyes."

"Certainly."

". . . You knew?"

"All along."

This led naturally to a discussion of the principle of Stringing-It-Out—holding back your revelations and surprises and confrontations for as long as possible and then, instead of dumping them in the reader's lap in one lump, letting the characters deal with them and react to them piece by piece. Most undergrad fiction writing moves too fast and too slow at the same time; it crawls along for pages and then suddenly too much happens at once.

—Have the students do a little writing in class whenever you can, especially whenever the opportunity arises to put one of the basic principles into practice. To hear is to forget; to see is to remember; to do is to understand.

EXPOSITION I My goat was got today for the first time this semester. Funny what gets you. I was droning on routinely about the importance of paying attention to details in writing, showing them how *nothing* is too trivial to fuss over. I read aloud a passage from someone's paper to demonstrate how awkward the *he/she* combination can be.

What right does he/she have to dismiss him/her for cheating when he/she himself/herself has probably cheated too?

A classic of its kind, and the student was not trying to be funny, believe it or not. I went on to explain that as you should write God instead of *god* even if you happen to be an atheist, you should write *he*—or *he or she* if it's absolutely necessary—even if you're a rabid feminist. (I didn't use the word rabid; I think I said dedicated.) Why? Because *god* and *he/she* call attention to themselves, are thus distracting, and will probably annoy those readers who disapprove of atheists and feminists.

"Of course, if your own atheism or feminism is the very point of the piece, then by all means write *god* and *he/she*."

"I am going to continue using he slash she," said Melissa Harkness, defiantly shedding her anonymity.

27

"Fine. That's entirely your choice. Any good editor will call you on it, however."

"In fact," she went on humorlessly, "I'm thinking of using she slash he."

At such moments the worst thing you can do is laugh; even crying is better.

Arguing with a student is like trying to review a John Hawkes novel—impossible to come to grips with the thing. I can only recall two or three occasions when a student became openly enraged at me. Five or six years ago one told me I was obnoxious and another that same semester quoted Shaw's memorable but essentially dumb line about those who can, do, those who can't, teach. In the one case I agreed that I was obnoxious (and kept on being obnoxious), and in the other I said that Shaw was undoubtedly right—by which deflectionary means I avoided hurling both students out the second-story window.

You can slip around these harsh little confrontations by being a respectful listener, ready to agree with whatever they say. Often what they accuse you of has a certain amount of truth in it, and so you're not necessarily being a spineless jellyfish in agreeing with them.

Never use sarcasm or irony. Play it straight all the way.

Monday, September 25

FICTION WORKSHOP Assignment due today: Three to five pages of dialogue, two people surprising each other, revealing their basic personalities. Some of the students read theirs aloud, with two evaluators apiece. The evaluators only had two minutes to talk and were thus forced to be more incisive and succinct than most of them would ordinarily be. The only instruction I gave them was "Tell the writer how the scene can be made more effective."

A note from Michelle Dupree yesterday afternoon in response to a sign posted all over Baker Hall:

The following faculty members are up for review for contract renewal: Gretchen Wylie, Janet Harper, Richard Geiren, Martin Russ. The English Department invites interested students to address evaluative comments in a memo to Dr. Alan Ogilvy by September 30.

Michelle, who has taken two of my courses, offered to speak out in my behalf, which is flattering since she's an unusually sharp senior and excellent all-around student who commands respect not only from peers but faculty. President of this, chairman of that, coordinator of the other. That she's African-black, extremely handsome, and the daughter of a college president doesn't hurt.

"I need some ammunition," she said on the phone last night.

I told her it would be uncool to do any horn-blowing on my own but suggested she pick up a copy of my *curriculum vita** from the departmental office. She also wanted to know by what criteria the promotions and tenure committee will be evaluating the four of us, and I found myself bitching to her about something that's bothered me for six years: No one pays attention to the quality of

* See pages 212–14.

teaching around here—no one but the students, that is. The student-written teacher/course evaluations are hauled out whenever a faculty member is up for review, but during my two-year stint on the committee hardly anyone did more than give them a glance. Student input in the deliberations is negligible.

Wednesday, September 27

EXPOSITION 1 The initial assignment was: "Bring in a 250-word piece on a subject of your choice. Make sure you say something *about* the subject, rather than merely describe and summarize." Many undergrads find it painfully difficult to write interpretively—that is, to give an opinion or at least assume a position outside the general consensus. Very few have ever been asked to declare themselves in print, and there's always a tremendous amount of consternation over this first assignment. For years their secondary school teachers demanded "English papers" and "English themes" and "book reports" from the poor little passives and they've cranked out hundreds of pages of material devoid of opinion or even general attitude. I've found that the best approach is to convince every undergrad that in his writing up to now he has been saying hardly anything at all; that when he printed MOMY I LOV YOU in crayon at the age of five he may have said more on the page than he has said since; and that the task now is to find out what he personally believes is important enough to write about.

For some students it's a nasty shock to run up against an instructor who demands personal opinion, and many go to great lengths to pretend not to understand what they're being asked to do. One of the ways to encourage them is to bring in examples of interpretive writing from newspapers and magazines—reviews and editorials, for instance. You need to assure them gently but persistently that they're not being asked to bare their souls or reveal anything even remotely intimate, but merely to convey an attitude toward whatever subject they choose to write about. By any means you can think of, prepare them for the traumatic experience of actually committing themselves in print to something, *anything*.

Many nonfiction teachers make the dumb mistake of providing subjects or topics. Let the student choose them himself, and make damn sure he says something *about* the subject—rather than merely turning in a description or summary or noncommittal analysis of it. Your refusal to provide subjects will drive some of them completely whacko, and occasionally a student will tell you in effect that he has an empty mind, that he has nothing whatever to say about anything in any way, shape, or form. Tell him you'll flunk him unless he coughs up an opinion or at least an attitude, and he will.

It's amazing how furiously they resist taking this first step. They'll ask you again and again to tell them what to write about. *Don't do it.* After they've chosen a subject at last they'll ask you to tell them what to say about it. *Don't do that either.* Most of the things they choose to write about in their first paper will be safe stock stuff: environmental pollution (they'll come out against it), honesty in government (they'll come out for it). Let them get away with that in the first paper, but not the second. They all need to learn that writing is an act of aggression, the moral equivalent of war.

Having to deal with undergrads on the emotional level is the only thing about teaching I find truly painful. At the beginning of each semester I have a sense of dread, knowing that I'm going to have to deal with the students' outrage when they realize the instructor is demanding not only a personal commitment but also a certain amount of self-revelation. Even after you've explained for the tenth time that all you're asking is for them to take a stand on something—anything!—many of them will behave as if you're trying to invade their privacy, even though it's only their anonymity you're trying to breach. You should invite the unhappiest students to your office, one at a time, and there try to convince them that you're neither a sadist nor a bully, but merely someone who wants to read something written by them as individuals (rather than something that was written by "one").

"But I *did* take a stand," said Frank Pellegrino, a rhinestone cowboy, whose first paper was about the torture of political prisoners in Chile.

I asked him how many people have taken a stand *for* the torture of political prisoners in Chile. That made him madder than he already was. "Are you saying I shouldn't even bother writing about it?"

"No, I'm saying that if you write about it you need to say something that hasn't already been said in every newspaper in the country."

"But it's an important issue."

"Of course it is—but is it important to you, personally?"

At first he was offended by the question, but a little later he admitted he had chosen it more or less at random, as something "significant" to write about for his first assignment. While he didn't come right out and say he was indifferent to the torture of political prisoners in Chile, he did admit that he wasn't seriously interested in the matter and because of his lack of interest the paper was boring. He used the word himself.

It's important to get the student to understand the enormous difference between what he thinks he's supposed to give a damn about and what he actually does give a damn about.

Here's the latest assignment: "Write a controversial or provocative or at least highly debatable 350-word statement, addressed directly and bluntly to me. There should be a clear Specific Purpose Statement at the beginning. After reading your statement I should be able to say that now I know something I didn't know before, or else that I now see something in a new perspective."

FICTION WORKSHOP Yesterday during the general discussion of Cindy Howarth's story, Ira Rosenberg observed that it was a piece of garbage. This is the sort of comment you're likely to hear during the early weeks, and you have to react swiftly and firmly so that it only happens once. You need to respond in a way that will reassure the writer that the story is by no means in the "trashal" category, while at the same time making sure not to offend the student who made the offending remark; in other words it's useful to hold a doctoral degree in diplomacy. If you fail to take swift action the first time such a remark is made the course will deteriorate into scheduled savagery and everyone will devote themselves to scratching at each other. This is far more likely to happen in a fiction workshop than anywhere else, since student fiction writers have to expose their innards and make themselves vulnerable in a way entirely unnecessary in any other field of undergraduate study.

Tell them it must be assumed that the writer has sweat blood over his story, has done the best he can, and now expects helpful feedback from his peers and the instructor. Tell them that the thing is to see how much stronger the story might be by revising it, not to talk about how awful it is in its present form. Then ask the students if they'll agree to avoid using provocative words such as garbage, asinine, ridiculous, absurd, stupid, and worthless. Point out that it's possible to convey a negative reaction in a positive way and that the effect is stronger in the long run. The students yesterday accepted this and were obviously relieved that a protective umbrella had been provided generally. After we had finished workshopping the story, Ira apologized to the (anonymous) student and added that after reconsideration he had decided it didn't belong on the trash heap after all.

Ira, by the way, is our workshop Strident. Most of the students seem either amused by his pop-off personality or else humorlessly hostile—except for Cindy Howarth, oddly enough. She seems to understand that he's not a willful troublemaker but merely a fellow determined to wrench an education out of this university. Often she gently supports him in his furious verbal probes, helping him to get his questions in focus. If I have a favorite student in the workshop it's Cindy, for no other reason than that she's a calming influence on Ira and his electrified Izzy. She has a kind face, something you don't run into very much around here.

I shouldn't have implied that undergrads in class are always on the verge of becoming a bloodthirsty mob. There is, however, a certain potential mob attitude that you would do well to keep in mind. After Ira's remark yesterday, for example, the class as a whole became highly animated and overexcited, almost rowdy, and it was necessary to "discipline" them with the suggestion that no one interrupt anyone else. This abrupt change in mood was the result of Ira's peace-destroying remark.

—Often a classroom of students will unconsciously follow a peer leader—a sarcastic put-down artist, for instance, who by dint of personality and precocious verbal skills will turn your course into a living nightmare unless you step in blandly and damp him off. My wife once said that at that age there's no charity: I would have said "no mercy." This particular mob attitude can work for you as well as against you. Sometimes the peer leader whom the students unconsciously imitate is a friendly, positively oriented creature. Michelle Dupree was one of those.

—Sometimes from out of the blue a student will ask a provocatively inane question very difficult to answer without a baseball bat. "Sounds like an interesting question," you can say. "Let's hear it again—and put it more succinctly, if you will." The more succinct version is usually silly-sounding enough that the other students, and often the questioner himself, will laugh, and the tension is harmlessly dispelled.

It's awfully easy to bully an undergrad but it's always a mistake.

—Another diplomatic problem that usually manifests itself early in the semester: A pair of students who mutter snide remarks to each other throughout the class, loud enough to break your concentration and everyone else's. You have to be careful dealing with this; if you stop and say something like, "Let's show a little consideration," you'll only remind the students of the eternal high school teacher, and their hostility nodes will be instantly titillated. Here's the technique I developed during my first semester of teaching, after I had swallowed my disgust at the realization that in teaching undergrads you're engaged in an adversary proceeding.

1. Look at the loudest of the back-row mutterers with your eyebrows raised, your expression conveying good-natured astonishment.

2. If that doesn't work, touch your lips with a finger and say Shh.

3. If these tactics don't work, ask the mumble leader for his opinion of the matter under discussion, making sure the question's appropriate and not intended to make a fool of him. Most undergrads feel generally foolish to begin with, in class and out, and you must scrupulously avoid saying anything that might confirm their self-opinion.

4. As a last resort you can say, "Sir, will I have to send you to the principal's office?" I've only had to go this far once and it worked; not only did the mumblers both chuckle along with the rest of the class, but they also came up afterward to apologize. Humor will save you in the end.

—I try to remain impersonal in class without being cold. Occasionally I'll offer a personal experience as an illustration, but only when it reveals a somewhat adverse facet of character. Yesterday in the workshop we were talking about the importance of revealing character through action, as opposed to merely telling the reader (as in "She was a compassionate person"); and I found myself talking about the time I was strolling down Fifth Avenue with Jack Reynolds and Paul Bacon when an elderly woman tripped and fell directly in our path. Jack sprang forward instantly to help her; Paul sprang backward in horror; the professor stood stunned and inactive. Thus we revealed something of our separate characters.

Friday, September 29

I recommend that you employ the peer-evaluation device whenever you can, in both your fiction and nonfiction classes. At least three good reasons for this. The student can develop his own critical skills while analyzing someone else's work; the student writer obtains several opinions on each story or essay or whatever; and it's a labor-saving device for the instructor. Here's the routine: Have them exchange papers in class. (Try to match up the clear thinkers with the fuzzies.) Ask them to answer—in writing—some questions designed to elicit helpful editorial suggestions (and incidentally to review some of the basic principles of good writing). Give them the option to do a second draft based on the peer evaluation. Tell them you'll collect the second draft at the next meeting. After you correct the second draft at home your problem is to convince them they need to do a *third* draft; but notice that all you've read so far is their second drafts (reading twenty first drafts can lead to suicidal depression, I have found).

Occasionally a student will take the option not to rewrite and, interestingly enough, it's almost always that student whose paper is in the worst shape. What this means is that he's afraid to come to grips with his own timidity. Invite him to your office and show him the fundamental flaw (never mind the details), which is almost always that the student has little to say and says it illogically. If he refuses to accept your suggestions—which is what happens in cases of extreme anxiety—assign your sharpest student to work with him on the rewrite.

EXPOSITION I I used this method with their letter-to-the-*Tartan* assignment. Here are the questions I asked them to answer (in writing):

1. Is there a *clear* Specific Purpose Statement, and does it appear at the start of the letter?

2. Is the letter written simply and straightforwardly, or is the style unnecessarily complicated and/or ambiguous? If the latter, specify the relevant passages.

3. Do you understand *exactly* what the writer is saying in every sentence, in every paragraph? If not, which passages are unclear?

4. Do the sentences and paragraphs follow one another logically? If there are any non sequiturs, cite them.

5. Is the writer specific enough, concrete enough? Or does he/she approach the subject in a general, abstract manner?

6. Are there any sweeping or too-broad statements that need support? If so, cite them.

7. Can you find any extraneous matter (verbal deadwood)? If so, cross it out.
8. Are there any statements so obvious that they needn't be stated at all? If so, cite them.
9. On the whole, is the letter very interesting, fairly interesting, or only somewhat interesting?
10. Does the letter present material with which most campus readers are already familiar—or does it offer something reasonably fresh (even if it's only a fresh twist to an old subject)?
11. Can the letter be strengthened in any other way? If so, make specific suggestions for a rewrite.

Sometimes, even after all this, a student will turn in a second draft so fouled up it'll take you longer to write your suggestions than it took him to write the piece itself. Simply make xerox copies (blanking out the signature), pass them out in class, and have the other students explain what's wrong in detail. Since most writing problems are common to all undergraduates (fuzzy thinking being the most prevalent) their in-class comments will be enlightening generally.

FICTION WORKSHOP Here is a useful bail-out procedure whenever you've been unable to make head or tails out of a story, or some important element of it. Pass the story out to everyone in class and ask the students to evaluate it. Collect their written evaluations at the beginning of the next workshop, then ask them to take out paper and pencil and answer a couple of questions—ostensibly to stimulate their critical phagocytes before the general discussion begins, but really to allow you a couple of minutes to look over the

39

evaluations. In a story we looked at last Wednesday, for example, the conflict *seemed* to revolve around a pair of sadomasochistic lesbian lovers, but even after three readings I wasn't sure what was coming off. By glancing through the evaluations I was relieved to find that the students were as confused as I was.

Monday, October 2

FICTION WORKSHOP Most of the stories so far have to do with lust-sex (as opposed to love-sex or even like-sex) and it's somewhat jarring to find oneself at forty-seven discussing with a straight face the fact that if "Jason" had indeed used a condom (the putting on of which Trissy Wolf has described for us in detail), then "Debi" would not have to walk around the campus for the rest of the day inconvenienced by the seminal fluids dripping down the inside of her thighs.

My wife doesn't understand how I can keep my face blank at such times.

During that discussion last Wednesday it was necessary to point out that the event described in the story (the clumsy deflowering of a freshman by her student advisor) would not in the ordinary course of events lead *necessarily* to instant lesbianism on the part of the disappointed "Debi."

"This encounter," explained the Buddha-faced instructor, "is after all not unlike that undergone by many, if not most, if not all—awkward, slightly ridiculous, unromantic, and minimally pleasurable gropings in the backseat of an old car."

To my enormous relief, the class did not burst into derisive laughter, and even seemed to agree with the point I was making: that if you must describe a more or less conventional event, make damn sure you give it an unconventional twist or slant. I was unaccountably tempted to quote the well-known sociologist, W. Allen: "Do you think sex is dirty?" "Yes, if it's done right." But there was no way to work it in—not when you are forty-seven and everyone else in the room is under twenty-two.

—In the first meeting of the semester, by the way, it's a good idea to offer your students the option of workshopping their stories anonymously. The instructor needs to know who wrote what, of course, but not really anyone else. The students are usually glad to have this option, to be able to sit there when it comes time for their story to get dumped on (which is exactly how many of them think of it) without their peers knowing who did the writing. More important from the instructor's point of view, the students are free to make the sharp or even rough comments that sometimes need to be made—whereas if everyone knows who wrote the story the remarks tend to be overpolite at the wrong time and are often so tentative as to be meaningless in a constructive sense.

Abigail Boretsky chose to sign her first story and paid the stiff price undergrads always pay whenever they do that. Although it was fine to be able to pin her down directly about her intentions, she was obviously in acute distress throughout the discussion. By the halfway mark she was flusteredly justifying this and defensively explaining that, and none of it was convincing. Her main objection was that we all misunderstood the theme of the tale, which— she informed us with charming hauteur—"is conveyed by the three fires, which symbolize Victor's need to destroy wealth." I was duty-bound to repeat, for the eighty-seventh time, the one concept that causes undergrads more consternation than any other: that the reader is entitled to know exactly what's going on at every point in the story. Even if the story is meant to be a series of mysteries, as some are, the reader needs to understand at least what it is that needs to be cleared up or not cleared up. If the story is meant to be a series of ambiguities, as many of the best are, the reader should at least be able to discern the alternatives. He should know who the people are, what they're doing or trying to do, what the symbols symbolize, and finally what the point of the whole mix is.

"The point," said Abigail with frost, "is that wealth corrupts."

Beryl Cooney asked her to show us where in the story this point is actually made.

"The story is meant to be read more than once. James Joyce said he expected his readers to devote a lifetime to *Finnegans Wake*."

I wanted to say "What readers?" since only seventeen have survived a single reading of the book—four literature professors, ten graduate students, two fond grandparents, and one madman—but you can't be flippant about Joyce unless you like living dangerously.

To tell Abigail I had read her story three times wouldn't have impressed her; it would only mean I had missed the point three times. She asked rhetorically if there existed a reader capable of fully understanding *Ulysses* in a single run-through. A good question. The answer is No—not fully comprehend every nook and cranny of the author's intention. On the other hand, it *is* quite understandable on first reading as a story about people. To put it rather crudely, you can enjoy the novel with no knowledge of Greek mythology.

You might think that in-class anonymity means a student can never defend his work against misunderstandings and foolish interpretations. No; any student who wants to can come and see you in your office, explain what needs to be explained, and allow you to pass the information along in the next class.

Wednesday, October 4

Yesterday our new chairman, Dr. Alan Ogilvy, called me into his office to say that the promotions and tenure committee has voted me out. On a scale of zero to three, four members voted 0, four voted 1, one voted 2, one voted 3. Dr. Ogilvy said that while my teaching and publication record had been judged satisfactory, my "administrative input left something to be desired." He wasn't able to explain what the committee meant by this. I asked if he'd find out for me and he said he would. I told him I was going to raise as much hell over the decision as possible. He warned me that in doing so I might lose my reputation. ("What reputation?") He mentioned a former colleague of his at Tulane who had sued the department after being denied tenure and has been unable to get another teaching job. He warned me that if I raised hell I might find it impossible to solicit letters of recommendation. Until then I had been outwardly calm, though burning coldly inside. "There's no one in this department I'd even *ask* for a letter of recommendation!" This was a sour grapes outburst, and not quite true—I'd ask Mildred Wilson and Stanley Urbanic.

The same committee voted me out three years ago, by the way, for even murkier reasons. I protested to the university's faculty review committee, the case was ordered reopened, the vote was overturned (thanks largely to the influence of Dean Atterbury), and I was reappointed.

I'm assuming that you're interested in the politics of a typical English department, since you mentioned the possibility of teaching full-time. My biggest mistake here has been to remain above the political aspect of the job, or perhaps I only mean the social.

Assuming that he or she teaches it competently and has published some fiction, it follows that a fiction-writing teacher has an unconventional mind, an unconventional point of view, and is therefore an unconventional person. The writer sees the glass as both half empty and half full (and if it's a glass of liquor it'll soon be empty). You may recall my saying that fiction writers are peculiarly tough but also peculiarly lame birds whose lameness forces on them an eccentric way of looking at the world. That's one reason why their written remarks are occasionally published— their way of seeing things is sometimes interesting enough for other people to want to read.

It's a cliché of pop psychology but true nonetheless that people often feel threatened in a general (and usually unconscious) way by a co-worker who is "different" and who sees things in a different way; and feeling threatened means becoming defensive; and if the threat is strong enough, that defensiveness can turn into a kind of indirect political aggression against the odd bird in the midst. I don't believe for an instant that anyone on the promotions and tenure committee has spiteful feelings toward me; but I do believe that the urge to get rid of me—a very strong one, considering the vote—is a defensive reaction of some sort. I'm not sure what it is about me that makes them so nervous; perhaps it's because I've published more original stuff over the past six years than all the rest of them put together. (I speak here only of quantity, not quality— although I do have a thought or two on that.) Perhaps it's only that I've made no friends in the department. I haven't been anti-social, you understand, merely nonsocial; and being a blank slate I've inadvertently given the colleagues an opportunity to concoct an image from their own imaginations. Over the years two relevant quotes have reached my ears, both summing up the essence of that image: "He's aloof" and "I've never even seen the inside of his house."

John McMasters, the former chairman, once told me with a sympathetically ironic smile that the 1975 vote might have gone in my favor had I "hosted at least one wine and cheese party." It's true that I've never invited a colleague into my house, nor have I ever wanted to; but it's also true that I've never invited *anyone* into my house, and that even my wife sometimes has a tough time getting in.

All else being equal, the fiction-writing teacher who can ingratiate himself with his colleagues is the one who will be reappointed.

I must say that of all the types and kinds and classes of people I've encountered over the years, literature professors and rhetoricians are the sorriest of the lot. After six years of peripheral but daily contact I've found them to be morally timid, petulant, unimaginative, joyless, insincere, petty, ineffectual, self-righteous, emotionally shallow, and thoroughly uncharitable. In general, they comprise a kind of secular priesthood—monklike creatures who lurk palely in academic cloisters, out of touch with the very life they're supposedly preparing their students to enter. Moreover, they read too many books.

If you succeed in getting a one-year appointment and then want to have your contract renewed, you must take the social ramble very seriously. Just tell yourself that you're gathering material, even though you'll soon discover that English professors are rarely worth writing about. You'll have to attend the occasional cocktail party and talk about literature and the latest Masterpiece Theatre production; you'll have to contribute two dollars occasionally to help buy flowers whenever someone goes to the hospital or a colleague's wife has a baby (a rare occurrence, for English professors are not much "into" children); and most important of all, you'll have to be ready at all times to stop and chat with your colleagues—rather than sweep blindly by as the natural writer tends to do (the self-induced trance being his normal state). Sweeping-by will be interpreted as arrogance or haughtiness or at least aloofness.

English professors, who should understand writers better than anyone, seem to understand them least.

One more unkind observation and I'll put this in the mail. When you meet your colleagues for the first time, you may find them quite the most charming group of people you've ever encountered; but ask yourself if you're not being dazzled by mere verbal skills—by technique rather than content. English professors are as a group probably the most facile conversationalists in the world; but they're readers and not doers, and will all be driven into the paddyfields when Pol Pot takes over.

Let me know if you want more of this kind of stuff, will you?

Thursday, October 5

FICTION WORKSHOP The first of yesterday's stories had to do with an adolescent boy trapped in a toilet stall by an insane janitor who is trying to break down the door and rape him. The boy escapes, only to fall into the hands of a harelipped harlot who rapes him with a pistol (if rape is quite the word for what occurs).

In dealing with such bizarre and plot-heavy stories in class, you won't always know whether the writer is putting you on or is dead serious. I've learned to assume he's serious. I got into trouble once by presuming that a student had dashed off a piece of stream-of-consciousness just before class in order to meet a deadline, and further presumed that everyone in the room recognized its worthlessness. Far from it! The piece turned out to be the result of several drafts of work, multileveled in meaning, heavy with Major Symbols, packed with allusions to classical mythology, all adding up to "a scathing indictment of

Christianity." The students found it worthy of the most serious consideration and I had the duty—one no true teacher can shirk—of convincing twenty young people that the piece was pretentious, pompous, and thoroughly amateurish. I failed, because I was too convincing, if you know what I mean. If I had had the sense to ask a series of gentle leading questions, the students would've been able to convince themselves of the worthlessness of the story, but this happened during my first semester of full-time teaching and I had as much to learn as the students.

I deserve a Nobel Prize for my diplomatic accomplishment in yesterday's class. It was as though I was chairing a meeting of an advisory council whose purpose was to establish the precise degree of sincerity in the text before us. I recall wondering aloud if perhaps the italicized words *El Endo* at the bottom of the last page "would seem to suggest the possibility that a highly subtle and complicated literary game is being played, with the reader as the worthy opponent." Did the other members of the council feel that this was remotely possible? The distinguished colleagues were reluctant to acknowledge the possibility until Bud Carr called into question the passage on page 6 in which the adolescent is described as staring down at the two turds afloat in the bowl, which are moving slowly in a counterclockwise direction. Conferee Carr wondered what the purpose of the passage might be. At this point the chairman, skateboarding on thin plywood, inquired rhetorically whether the turds might possibly represent life itself. The council chamber rang with raucous laughter, and the chairman, ever conscious of decorum, stared blandly at the distinguished conferees until order was restored. After that the way was clear for some deeply cutting remarks, for Mark Grabowski, the writer, had laughed as hard as anyone.

Yesterday's class was one of the most animated I can recall, probably due to a certain emotional tone sounded at the outset when Dinah Bernstein complained that I had failed to protect Monci Jo Nickerson from attack in the previous class. There had apparently been a general discussion of this since our last meeting and Dinah had been appointed to broach the matter.

A little background. Monci Jo's story was closer to the professional level than anything we've had so far: a twenty-six-page tale about a lonely middle-aged woman looking for a friend, finding a lover briefly, getting pregnant, learning that the lover has only been kind to her out of pity and wants no part of parental responsibility. The discussion last Monday seemed even-handed; no one said anything remotely unkind—not even Ira Rosenberg, who often works himself into a trembling twitching frather in his frustration over being forbidden to tear everyone's work apart. Nevertheless, Monci Jo called me at home on Monday night to say that she was "extremely disturbed" over the comments in class. We had a long talk in my office on Tuesday, but she was not at all comforted to learn that *most* students are extremely disturbed by the comments in class, that it's natural to be in turmoil afterward, that the unconscious mind will sort it all out eventually, that whatever comments are useful will stick and the rest will disappear. She didn't come right out and say so but there's little doubt that it was my comments in particular that offended her. My heaviest criticism was that she has a strong tendency to write Literature, to be pseudopoetic, to use words like contemn and plaint and ineffable and ineluctable too much. It turns out that Monci Jo was not merely disturbed but devastated by the whole business. She cut all her classes yesterday. And now here's Dinah Bernstein accusing me of failing to protect our still presumably anonymous waif from attack.

In such situations the teacher must never do what his emotions urge him to do—that is, leap forward with all sorts of self-justification. No; calmly open up the subject for general discussion, sit back and listen, inserting leading questions from time to time, so that the students can blow off their steam. They'll work out their own confusion and resentment and then, having relieved themselves emotionally, will begin to address the situation reasonably. Assuming that your comments on the story were valid and fair and intended kindly, the students will now proceed to convince themselves of it. The instructor remains neutral throughout all this, like a psychiatrist at a stormy group-therapy session. It was Greta Nyquist who turned the tide by saying it's not the instructor's duty to protect anyone's ego. She was wrong, but that didn't matter then. Abigail Boretsky then said she too had been treated rather roughly when we workshopped her first story and that her feelings had been hurt, but that she had gotten over it within a week and now believes the experience was a positive one. Jennifer Balle put the cap on it by saying the instructor had been tactful in his remarks about the twenty-six-page story and had in fact made it plain he thought highly of it. At this point the instructor offered to plight his troth to Ms. Balle, a suggestion juvenile enough to tickle a key rib or two and dissolve the remaining tension.

After it was all over I told them that professional editors are going to be much rougher on their work, and that a fiction workshop is a good psychic training ground for the sort of blunt feedback you can expect in the marketplace: "Your story works except for the contrived ending"; "Your opening chapter is extraneous"; "Your protagonist is two-dimensional."

Greta Nyquist (a short round rumpled party in pigtails, enormous mischievous eyes behind hornrims) came to the office after yesterday's class to say that Monci Jo is still so upset that Greta is worried about her. Monci Jo sat beside Ira Rosenberg in Monday's class and according to Greta was literally afraid he was going to hit her as he commented on her story.

You asked how one's teaching is evaluated by the department. It isn't—not really. The students are asked to fill out a teacher/course evaluation in the final class, and when a teacher comes up for review, the chairman and a few members of the promotions and tenure committee leaf through them, but rarely if ever do they interview seniors and alumni, which is the way I think it ought to be done. I admit that this absence of true evaluation bugs me more in a personal sort of way than in a philosophical or socially conscious way. It bothers me that none of my colleagues, including the various chairmen and deans, have ever shown the slightest interest in what goes on in my classroom. It bothers me too that applicants for teaching jobs here (and almost everywhere else) are never auditioned. For some cockeyed reason it is assumed that if you have the required degree you can therefore do an adequate job of teaching. It goes without saying that one of the reasons a college or university exists is to educate young people—that is, for the purpose of teaching students; and yet in one institution of higher learning after another you'll find that it's only the students themselves who pay any attention to the quality of the teaching. In our department, for instance, that the students thought highly of their teachers meant nothing in the end: Many were fired because their publication record was skimpy. I have yet to meet a student who came to Carnegie-Mellon because he or his parents were impressed by something published by a member of our department.

In answer to your question about minorities and so on: There are only a handful of black students in the College of Humanities and Social Sciences; I've never had more than two in any course, and it's usually one or zero. In my experience, poor writers among the students—black, white, brown, red, or yellow—all have the same fundamental problem: fuzzy thinking. You have to work very hard to convince such students that it's in their own interest to think their ideas through before committing them to paper. For the instructor this usually means correcting several drafts of each assignment. For obvious reasons, many of the black students are likely to become especially angry at you for making them rewrite and rewrite, and occasionally you'll run into an "activist" who will accuse you of oppression or worse. I've heard the word "genocide" used in this connection, believe it or not—the implication being that a certain instructor was a kind of imperialist bent on expropriating black students' souls.

The only black student I have at the moment is Velma Brown, and already I'm in hot water with her. She refuses to accept any criticism of her work. In her view there's no possibility whatever that anything she has written can be improved and, furthermore, all her friends agree with her—or so she tells me. In fact, every line of her written work desperately cries out for revision. After she refused to rewrite her first paper I sent her down to the Communication Skills Center with a note ("I've been unable to convince Ms. Brown that her paper can be improved"), but the staff member who handled the case allowed himself to be intimidated by Velma's combined Black Power/Women-Can-Do-It-on-Their-Own routine, and there's still no rewrite. My next move was to ask Velma to bring the paper to class: I intended to ask Melissa Harkness to work with her on it privately, but Velma triumphantly claimed that she had lost it.

"That's too bad," I said sincerely, sympathetically, and sadistically. "Knock me off another, will you? Three pages, due Friday."

She was shocked into silence, and I scurried away while there was still time.

In other words, I can't answer your question. Every black student I've encountered has been intensely and defensively conscious of being Black, understandably so. Unfortunately, it is only the rare ones like Michelle Dupree who seem able to suppress the ideological and emotional anger long enough to concentrate wholeheartedly on educating themselves.

Friday, October 6

Late last night Lucy and I suddenly realized that if my firing is confirmed we'll be able to get out of Pittsburgh at last—and maybe even be able to return to the land where vultures hover at noon and coyotes howl at midnight. Northeast born and bred, both of us, but Far West in spirit. Suddenly society in the Northeast strikes us as formal, structured, prissy, impenetrable (for us), while in the West it seems by comparison so tolerant and flexible and friendly and fleabitten. Neighbors and co-workers don't get huffy so easily if you're not like them.

EXPOSITION I I handed back the "corrected" assignments today, every one of them needing a rewrite. V. Brown, as she signs herself, realizing that she now owes me *two* rewrites, tottered after me down the hall in shoes that clacked.

"Mister, you've attacked every damn sentence I've turned in. How do you expect me to get an education when you attack every sentence?"

"Attack isn't the word, Ms. Brown. I'm only trying to show you that some passages can be strengthened."

"You did it again—you attacked my sentence!"

"Haw?"

"You said attack wasn't the right word. I can't even open my mouth!"

"Let's go to my office and talk it over."

But she whirled, nearly falling, and went clacking away, a tall good-looking girl in a gray dress. You might think I've lost her; but I've been through this before. V. Brown has crossed me off her list; and Monci Jo Nickerson, I'm told, is still sulking in her room. They'll be back.

—You can only teach writing to someone who is interested. Many undergrads come to your classes completely uninterested in learning how to write well or even

54

learning to write better. Usually it's because they don't understand how useful the ability to write simply and clearly will be when they launch themselves into the crowded, impatient, intolerant world. How can you get them interested? Tell them that college graduates who can write simply and clearly are so rare nowadays that employers single them out for special attention.

It's quite true that fiction can't be taught; but you can pass along a few shortcuts and get them interested in the craft of it. I don't think any student wastes his time in a good fiction workshop, not even the talentless ones. By the end of the semester they'll have developed their critical skills to some extent, will respond more deeply to literature, will know a bit more about human nature than they did at the start. It may not be much, but how many other English courses achieve more?

FICTION WORKSHOP Some typical writing-student problems:

1. Undergrads tend to use more words than they need to, and much of your work involves showing them that a certain word or phrase or sentence or paragraph can be deleted without loss. Since students are so sensitive to criticism, the best way is to enclose the deletable passage in red-ink brackets and scribble *Is this essential?* alongside it. Notice that this question is somewhat more tactful than *Is this necessary?*—which conveys a slight air of impatience.

2. More often than not, the opening paragraph of a student story is little more than a sort of warming-up, a setting-of-the-scene or mood (usually in the form of a detailed description) and can be deleted. Often too the student will begin his story in a superliterary manner,

coming on like an Author using a quill pen. Try to get him to start spinning the actual yarn in the first sentence ("Simba roared").

3. Many undergrads resent having to write fiction in the traditional mode and will accuse you of unfairly restricting their talent by your reactionary insistence that the characters be recognizably human; that the emotional progression of the story has a beginning, a middle, and end; that the action occurs in a recognizable setting; that the story has a point—or at least that the reader can discern some attitude toward the material, even if it's only a vague "indictment of society." This last requirement is the one that drives them up the wall, for many would prefer to write pointless stories. Whenever someone wants to argue about this, all you have to do is point out that the reader should never be allowed to say *So what?* or *Who cares?* after he has finished the story. This they buy.

These requirements *are* restrictive, but without them many students would turn in sketches and moody static stuff about trees that dwell in mystical communion with their sister the wind. Which would be all right except that such stuff is impossible to comment on, pro or con, and the students instantly defend it as experimental or innovative fiction. Experimental fiction is fun because it's so easy, and you have the illusion not only that you're writing Literature but that you're actually expressing yourself (Idea for bumper sticker: HELP STAMP OUT SELF-EXPRESSION). Over at the Hillman Library there's a tree stump with an arrow stuck in it, which the library officials refer to as a work of art. This is encouraging to the masses, since it implies that anyone can create art; but what the masses don't know is that hardly anyone can write interestingly about interesting people doing something interesting.

Warn your students that you will punish severely anyone who dares turn in stream-of-consciousness fiction. Reason: It's too easy, and, more important, such a piece from an undergrad invariably contains neither story nor character other than the sleep-inducing, out-of-gear mind of the narrator.

4. The most prevalent problem in student fiction writing is lack of plot or suspense or drama. Usually plot is what your protagonist does or tries to do and how much trouble he has at it and how he and everybody else reacts to it. In most student stories he does too damn little and doesn't have enough trouble doing it and nobody else much cares, because there's so little at stake. In most student stories the protagonist is a wimp (popular undergrad word this semester). Funny thing, though—if you bitch too loudly about this in class, your students will assume you want cheap melodrama: Steve McGarrett of *Hawaii Five-O* rescuing the governor's fashion-model daughter from the clutches of a Maoist madman. You might try telling them that in the best (orthodox) playwriting the author gets his protagonist stuck up a tree in Act I, has the antagonist throw rocks at him in Act II, and gets him down in Act III. It sounds good and may shut them up awhile.

Bud Carr, who at twenty-one has read more of the world's great literature than I have, stunned me in my office yesterday by announcing that the development of fiction ended with the publication of *Ulysses*.

"I consider it my artistic duty to break new ground," he said, glaring at me under the bill of his yellow "Cat" cap. "I intend inventing a new form of fiction."

On automatic pilot I defended the conventional form

by claiming that it's open-ended and flexible and infinitely spacious enough for the writer to say or do damn near anything he wants.

"What I'm interested in," he explained very patiently, "is creating form independent of substance."

I've had this conversation with many students, and so will you. Basically what's happening is this: The student is telling you that he has given up trying to write stories about people because he can't find anything to say about them, and wants your blessing as he launches a new student career of writing words about words.

Give him nothing. This is a crucial moment in his life. If you let him go he's likely to end up with a doctoral degree in rhetoric and will spend the rest of his life teaching undergrads how to write words about words. The best thing to do is to put him up against the wall and threaten to shoot him if he doesn't shut up with that silly stuff.

5. Most undergrad fiction writers work hard to keep the security blanket of obscurity pulled tightly around them. Be careful whenever you call a student on this: He'll clutch and claw that blanket to himself with perfect ferocity, citing Kafka and Joyce and Beckett and Pinter and Genêt and Hawkes and so on. Telling him that those fellows always know exactly what it is they're obscuring, and why, won't do the trick since no student is going to admit he's obscuring a vacuum. You're in for a terrific battle if you insist that he make clear what the story is about; the last thing he wants to admit is that he hasn't the vaguest idea. I recommend that you demonstrate, using examples from world literature, that a writer can be delicate and subtle, eloquent and profound, in a way that is direct and clear and simple. They will still prefer to imitate the

style of *Finnegans Wake*, but you may plant a wild seed here or there.

Undergrads generally consider Kafka, Joyce, Beckett, etc., more deserving of serious regard than Faulkner, Hemingway, Fitzgerald, Steinbeck, Cheever, Updike, Bellow, Malamud, Singer; this has to do largely with the degree of obscurity in the former and the lack of it in the latter. The reason why undergrads are enamored of obscurity is that there's no easier or more Literary way of hiding absence of substance, attitude, commitment, and content.

I only know that in fiction today less and less is being said more and more impressively.

Monday, October 9

Jill Jones and Roxie Kennard, both seniors and former students of mine, came around today to ask if it's true I've been fired.

"But *why?*" asked Roxie.

"Something about administrative input, or rather the lack of it."

"Meaning what?"

"I haven't generated any programs."

"Half the faculty seems to be generating programs," said Roxie, looking disgusted. "Why do they need *you* to do it?"

"Well, the folks in Warner Hall are mighty impressed with program generators," I said, trying to remain neutral.

"Sure," said Jill, "even when the programs are no darn good."

"Haven't you generated *any* programs?" asked Roxie.

"I generate nothing outside of the classroom except babies."

"Some of us are thinking of dropping out in protest."

"Do what?"

"Some of the English majors are talking about transferring, either to other departments or to other schools."

"That's kinda drastic—just because one teacher gets fired."

A compliment or two was paid and comparisons with other teachers were made. I told them I was glad they felt that way about me but that they were wrong about the other teachers. "And I haven't left *yet*, you know."

"You won't be around next year."

"Don't be too sure. I went through all this three years ago . . ." And I told them about the firing in 1975, the letters to the *Tartan*, the appeal to the faculty review committee, the reappointment. They wanted to know if I'm going to go the same route again.

"I don't know yet."

They said they wanted to do something to keep me on and asked for suggestions. I said it wouldn't be cool for me to suggest anything.

"Can we write letters?"

Remaining neutral isn't easy when someone is trying to find a way to help you. I had several suggestions but if I had made them, word would have gotten around that

Professor Russ was using the students to promote his cause. I'd love to *use* them that way—but it would be too much like a psychoanalyst seducing patients. The only thing I did was agree that writing letters to Dean Atterbury might not be a bad idea.

—V. Brown and Monci Jo Nickerson were both present in class today—the former sizzling in the back row in Exposition, the latter plathing radiantly in the front row in Workshop, proud to have survived her ordeal so far. I expect more crises.

EXPOSITION I I handed out copies of a book review and asked the students to read it carefully and then briefly list the reviewer's ideas. "Note that you're being asked to list the *reviewer's* ideas," I warned them. "Not Hermann Hesse's ideas."

Here are the first two paragraphs of the review, to give you the flavor:

In *Steppenwolf*, Hermann Hesse explores the dichotomy that exists in the soul of one Harry Haller. On the one hand, he seems to say, we have an individual enamored of the order and security of the bourgeois world, while on the other we have a "Steppenwolf"—a man painfully insulated from society. Hesse's storytelling technique is so remarkable as to seduce all but the most passive of readers. Starting with his own curious observations regarding Haller's mode of existence, the writer follows his own involvement until the unwary reader is trapped. One struggles in vain to imagine a reader whose outlook could remain intact after undergoing the stunning experience provided by this superb novel.

For this reviewer the experience was unique. As Hesse introduced me to the phenomenon called Harry Haller, it seemed as though I was confronting a projection of myself, no

61

less, in twenty years; and yet one cannot escape the conclusion that Hesse's purview encompasses all of mankind . . .

It goes on like that for three pages—nothing but hot air, a sort of academic snow job. No stand is taken, beyond the one-sided adulation: Nothing is interpreted. Any critical judgments to be found in the piece derive from Hesse himself rather than the reviewer. He *seems* to say something here and there, as when he calls the storytelling technique remarkable, but there are no examples to show us why it's remarkable and so the statement is almost meaningless (in the sense that *The sun is shining* is a "So what?" statement if there's no context). He says that reading the novel was a unique experience, without indicating what was unique about it. He says that Harry Haller is a projection of himself in twenty years, without telling us enough about himself for the statement to have any meaning.

After they turned in their lists I told them that I had tricked them, that I wrote the piece especially for the course, knowing they'd assume it must be a worthy and serious piece of writing if a professor handed it out in class. There was a ripple of delighted laughter, but a few of the students were quite unamused and one or two insisted that the piece contained some ideas. We went over it line by line, me trying to show them the important difference between a statement of fact and an idea.

Frank Pellegrino asked, rather belligerently, what the purpose of the exercise was. In the usual bland way I explained that too many students had been turning in academic snow jobs, and rather than go to the trouble of scheduling private conferences to deal with the matter I decided to write a sort of unfunny parody and see how many recognized it for what it was—a worthless piece of writing devoid of true ideas. Only three out of eighteen did, and so the point was made indirectly.

Taking advantage of their momentarily stunned condition, I asked them to reread the final sentence ("It is impossible for this reviewer to divorce himself from Hesse's entrotypical philosophy long enough to evaluate the novel objectively; one can only bow humbly in the direction of an artist all too clearly a master of light and shadow.") and warned them that in doing their next assignment—a review of *Miss Lonelyhearts*—they are to avoid this sort of intimidated apology.

"Your duty is to come directly to grips with the work, whether it's *The Iliad, Paradise Lost, Moby Dick*—or *Miss Lonelyhearts*. Appraise it with an eye as cold as that of any professional critic. Reviewing isn't summarizing or analyzing alone; it's also telling the reader what you think of the work. And don't think that calling Miss Lonelyhearts 'a Christ figure' is going to do the job. Obviously he's 'a Christ figure'—but so what? Who was Christ, and what do *you* mean by Christ figure?"

They all looked haggard at the bell and thoroughly put-upon as I bullied my way out the door.

FICTION WORKSHOP Trissy Wolf is the kind of overfussy student writer you're likely to run up against next semester. Here's a sample of her stuff:

"Indeed," she assayed, as she smoothed out the pleats of the Givenchy she had purchased the day before and which she wore now with more than a touch of panache as she sat there drumming her carmine-colored fingernails on the ceramic-tile surface of the elegant poolside cabana table.

In such writing the characters are always uttering tiny little remarks and having tiny little perceptions while performing aimless movements with their hands in a veritable whirlwind of stage business.

In Bud Carr's story, which we looked at yesterday, a character spends an inordinate amount of time "tracing the patterns of the cracks on the table top" with his fingers, and when Dinah Bernstein called this into question there followed a general discussion about the possible sexual symbolism. I managed to work in that a symbol is no damn good unless the reader can recognize what it symbolizes—and why do you need a symbol anyway when the real thing is just as good and usually better? Undergrads have no patience with this line of thought, and it was with an air of smug condescension that Bud informed me after class that the fingers in the cracks symbolized the protagonist's homosexual interest in the waiter.

"Ah, of course," I said. "Should have seen that."

My meager diplomatic skills were called into play more than once yesterday. The students objected when I suggested that a line from Bud's story—*Marlene had hips, large grape-jelly hips all smooth and sweet*—left something to be desired and it wasn't Marlene. I was forced to point out that grape jelly, while it is indeed smooth and sweet, is also purple and sticky and therefore not necessarily the best metaphor with which to convey Marlene's attractiveness, which *was* the author's intent.

"Can't the line imply hips grown large from having eaten too much grape jelly?" asked Abigail Boretsky.

"Now that is an interesting possibility."

Because the phrase "grape-jelly hips" has a certain literariness about it the students preferred to appreciate it. I preferred to appreciate it myself, actually, recognizing that Bud had at least reached for something beyond the ordinary, even though it didn't work.

If you don't have a perverse sense of humor, a taste for poker-faced silliness, and infinite patience, you will bonk out midway in your semester. God intended for most nineteen- and twenty-year-olds to be naïve and write badly; you can't criticize them for being normal, if you know what I mean.

Sometimes I suspect that writing is actually being taught in my classes—but not very often. Certain alumni have assured me that I did indeed teach them how to write, but I'm always skeptical. It's something like having your grown children thank you for teaching them how to speak English: You had something to do with it, to be sure, but mostly they taught themselves.

Terence O'Haggarty's story had to do with a horny fellow going up and down in an elevator, the elevator itself turning out to be a veritable riot of sexual symbols. Although I acknowledged the cleverness of the conceit, I was forced to ask if it wasn't a "So what?" situation. I hated to do it. Yes, the elevator shaft is vaginalike, yes the elevator itself is penislike, yes the control panel is clitorislike (sort of) but what are we to make of a clitoris inside of a penis, of a—

"Can't a writer have some fun?" asked Terence, merry eyes dancing.

"Fun? *Fun*, you say?" (It was like the Cookie Monster being asked to share a cookie: "Share?")

65

I was literally saved by the bell.

"We will discuss Fun at our next meeting."

Undergrad fiction writers are intensely interested in the possibilities of metaphor, simile, alliteration, allusion, parallelism, symbolism, and all the other literary devices. Which is fine. The problem is that they're more interested in the devices themselves than in using them effectively. You get the impression that certain students sit down at the typewriter with the conscious intention of employing seven metaphors, three similes, five alliterations, two allusions, one parallelism, and three Major Symbols before deciding what the story's about. You might try to convince them that the devices will take care of themselves if they concentrate principally on the emotional struggles of the characters; but most undergrads prefer to think of fiction writing as something for academic consideration and are comfortable in the belief that the cart is more important than the horse.

For student writers one of the most difficult problems is "creating character"—and it's a damned hard thing to teach. Many undergrads don't even understand the concept of character, and one way of starting from scratch is to point out the surface differences between the students themselves: Bud Carr's "Cat" cap and Vandyke; Mark Grabowski's blond ponytail; Terence O'Haggarty's merry eyes. I stopped with the boys because it would be difficult to point out the girls' salient physical characteristics or even habits of dress without stepping on a toe or two: Greta Nyquist, though quite attractive, *is* short and round; Cindy Howarth's lovely kind face *is* plain; Jennifer Balle is angelic-looking but she *does* have an aggressive nose—and so on. Abigail Boretsky, on the other hand, is a beauty but a flawed beauty, and how can you explain that that's the best kind? I asked for a few words about any student in the room, words defining his or her individuality, but had to choke that off when Beryl Cooney started in on Trissy Wolf. Trissy is a rural-rooted girl who seems to have exchanged her eyeglasses for contact lenses, and doesn't seem to notice the smoldering glares she gets from women's movement activists like Beryl who deplore her sudden attempt to turn herself into a sex object. Trissy works hard to keep her head-by-Revlon above water academically and you can see her struggling bravely to overcome her feeling of inferiority, sitting there among the urban sophisticates.

It's useful to try getting them to think in stereotypes— or at least recognizable, definable types. Too many characters in student fiction are indeterminate, with the reader unable even to tell what *kind* of people they are. You can explain that while it's poor form to end up with a stereotype in your final draft, it's helpful to think in stereotypes as you're assembling your cast (giddy housewife, macho blowhard, uncompromising man of character, obnoxious brat, wise granddad, and so on); then you can sort out and balance the characters against one another—can orchestrate them.

The matter of orchestrating. You need to pound this concept into their heads as early in the workshop as possible. Beryl Cooney's first story was about some ladies at a bridge party and every last one of them was middle-aged, overweight, overly made up, overmanicured, overtalkative; they were all silly and vapid and insensitive and materialistic; they all had empty souls and led empty lives. Beryl was primarily interested in making an ideological point and wasn't at all interested in whether it was a good story or not, but it gave me an opportunity to lecture on the need for orchestration of characters.

Students understand the concept readily enough if you provide examples from stories they admire. If they give you a hard time about stereotypes you might point out that most of the characters from the great movies are in a certain sense stereotypes: Humphrey Bogart in *Casablanca*, Marlon Brando in *Streetcar Named Desire*, Vivien Leigh in *Gone With the Wind*, Gary Cooper in *High Noon*, Bette Davis in *The Little Foxes*, and so on. (Most English majors are film freaks.) Years ago you could convey the concept of orchestration by using the term in its original musical sense—showing the students how in a big-band arrangement the tune was passed around between the different banks of instruments with a solo now and then, the tune having a different flavor each time it changed hands. Such an obvious analogy would make little impression on most undergrads nowadays, since rock music has comparatively little by way of orchestration.

Tuesday, October 10

EXPOSITION 1 I'm wallowing in a warm bath of self-satisfaction right now, having just finished reading the revised versions of the third assignment. Without exception they're in far better condition than the originals. The sloppy thinkers have begun to accede to the demand for carefully thought-out sentences and paragraphs and are generally taking more pains with their writing. From now on there will be less and less struggling between instructor and student on the emotional level. I look forward to returning these papers, for I've scratched hundreds of encouraging and reinforcing comments on them.

Wednesday, October 11

Glad you're finding "the other stuff" interesting; I wasn't sure if you wanted straight facts or impressions or suggestions or what. In answer to your question about the vultures and coyotes: I was referring to the Napa Valley, north of San Francisco. We spent the summer there, on Mount St. John, overlooking the Robert Mondavi vineyards. We were caretakers, and what we took care of was a vegetable garden, fourteen chickens, three geese, a dog, and a cat. (The most surprising thing about the summer was discovering that we have an insane family passion for chickens.) No, we have no serious plans to move there. In case the faculty review committee doesn't come to the rescue this time, I've applied to three schools with openings for someone more or less like me—as indicated by their notices in the Associated Writing Programs bulletin. Frankly, it would be a relief to get out of the teaching game altogether; you get tired of hearing yourself say the same damn things over and over. And we would be delighted to get out of Pittsburgh itself, if it comes to that; it's not a place where Lucy and I care to grow old and die and get buried in.

Back to business. Here's a couple of small suggestions. Never try to be "with it" or use Now-slang in class; it's probably already out of date by the time you hear it. Some slang becomes accepted generally, of course (being uptight and into something are approaching it), but wait until you're sure before using it. Heavy, super, and dynamite were Pittsburgh youth words about two years ago, but it seems as though they're following nitty-gritty and letting the good times roll (as well as all hang out). It's best to talk in a conversational, colloquial manner in class, giving yourself a one-second tape delay for purposes of self-editing. Remember that you're giving a performance as well as teaching a class, and there's no reason at all why you have to be yourself. Why not be someone else?

I was reminded again today of the importance of entertaining undergrads in the classroom if you expect them to learn anything. Chip Bowers and Sharon Dworak dropped by the office to complain that they're not learning anything in Professor Stanley Urbanic's technical writing course.

"Not *anything?*"

"Zilch."

I let them talk it out as thoroughly as they wanted to, and got the impression that Professor Urbanic has already taught them plenty but that his colorless methods have led them to believe otherwise. He's one of the three or four colleagues I'm sure are effective in the classroom (there are twenty-six of us in the department). The man has had two heart attacks, has not been looking well lately, and is, I imagine, even less colorful than usual. Nevertheless, it's my impression that he's the best writing teacher we have. Because he works slowly (but thoroughly) and without dialectics or drama and does no wooing at all, a few of the younger students try to convince themselves each year that he's incompetent.

"He shuffles into the classroom like an old-time German professor," Sharon complained. "Doesn't say good morning or even look at us. Delivers his material. Walks out when the bell rings. That's it."

I know Sharon and Chip well enough ("Hi! I'm Sharon. This is Chip. We're lovers.") to be openly irritable with them ("I know, damn it—you told me last semester."), so I bombarded them with blunt questions about the course, hardly giving them time to answer; and then when they left an hour later they had convinced themselves that Professor Urbanic had already taught them a few things they need to know.

Me, I'd prefer to learn almost anything from a teacher who comes on like an old-time German professor, one of those *Whoever has ears, listen; whoever doesn't, buzz off* types; but students do a lot of not-listening in class, and I'm reminded of the old joke about the man who uses a plank to get his mule's attention. You do need to get their attention before anything else, and it's helpful to be a bit of a ham actor: sudden exclamations, violent gestures, startling colloquialisms, demented chortlings, menacing twitches, grotesque throat-clearings, and the like. The students will stare at you, helpless mice in the presence of a king cobra, wondering when you're going to strike and definitely wondering what you're going to do or say next. At least you'll have their attention. In short, one needs to be a combination of Maria and Charlie Callas in the classroom.

71

FICTION WORKSHOP Greta Nyquist wrote one of today's two stories, and what a delight it was to discuss a student story that's just fine the way it is (not counting a few minor points). When such a story shows up, you should praise it as elaborately as you can—not simply to encourage the writer (a true writer needs no encouragement and can't be discouraged) but also to assure the students in general that you're not the negatively oriented put-down artist many of them thought you were.

Thursday, October 12

FICTION WORKSHOP I read them a short passage from Crane's "The Open Boat" (about the dying soldier of the legion) to introduce the concept of the importance of *sound* in writing, and to encourage them to begin listening to their own stuff.

—I encourage you to read aloud to your classes as often as possible, especially when you find something illustrating a point you've been trying to make. You may be touched at the childlike way they listen. Sometimes I feel like Dad reading *Goodnight Moon* to twenty toddlers in Dr. Dentons. Last Monday I read the opening chapter of Maugham's *Of Human Bondage*. Less than three pages long, it exemplifies a good many of the basic principles of conventional-traditional-orthodox fiction. Everything happens in scene form—like scenes in a film (no exposition, no explanation); you're told nothing, shown everything.

And he relates his tale in the simplest and most direct manner possible. There's no sense of the Artist creating Art or an Author creating Literature. There's no "style" to distract your attention from what's happening on the screen, so to speak. He doesn't stop to describe anything— except a word or two in passing—and yet you see the "sets" in question (a sickroom, a hallway) with perfect clarity. The principle here is that unless the background is unusual, all you need to do is indicate it lightly in passing and the reader will dress his own set. Too much description and the reader gets confused, frustrated, and finally bored. If you want to introduce a ravishingly beautiful woman into your narrative, she'll be all the more ravishing if you give the reader nothing but a sort of silhouette and allow him to fill it in with his own version of Beautiful. Excuse me if I seem to be telling you something you already know; I'm only trying to alert you that it's something the students don't know.

Fiction-writing students would much rather describe than narrate. Would rather tell than show. Would rather summarize than dramatize. Would rather explain than demonstrate. Would rather obscure than clarify. I don't know why it is (something to do with Satan, I suppose), but students seem to want to do everything wrong.

A word about style. Students are fascinated by style, and expect the instructor to spend a lot of time talking about it. To feed this hunger I've collected some twenty-five definitions. After the students have read them they agree that they all say basically the same thing: Style is the way a writer writes, line by line, paragraph by paragraph. The thing can in no wise be taught, or even self-taught; it's something that develops on its own like the sound of your voice as you grow up. Even though it can't be forced, most students try anyway, which almost always means imitating the style of a currently admired writer. In the days when such writers as Maugham and Cather and Hemingway and Salinger were models, no one got into too much trouble; but nowadays it's Robert Coover, John Barth, John Hawkes, Donald Barthelme, Thomas Pynchon, and their ilk—their writing is heavy on style, light on content. With such models the student writer has little incentive to say anything, or even to make sure his story is about anything. Language for the sake of language and form for the sake of form are the thing now, and rhetoricians are more concerned with language than what it's used for.

Friday, October 13

EXPOSITION 1 By now every student in class can tell the difference between the interpretive approach and the straight-fact approach. Most of them realize that their "book reports" and "English themes" were noninterpretive. Even though they understand the difference, at least half of them will turn in a description or summary or an uncritical analysis of *Miss Lonelyhearts*. For most of them this is the first time anyone has asked them to do some independent thinking, and a few can't believe that's what I want.

—You asked about giving grades. My policy is peculiar: I only give a mid-term and a final grade, and that only because I have to. If you slap a grade on every assignment, as most instructors do, you'll have to fight off hordes of

74

undergrads demanding to know why Debby got a C on last week's paper and Kathy a D, even though it's perfectly evident that Kathy's paper is of higher quality. While it may be true that some papers with lower grades *are* occasionally in better shape, comparatively, the student writer is in competition with himself and not his classmates. This *is* explainable, if the students pin you down on it, but it takes about ten hours.

Here's a typical line of development, paper by paper, from the start of the course to the final exam, assuming an ideal student: horrible; rotten; not as rotten; much better than your horrible first paper; much better than your rotten second paper; not bad but not good either; good but not good enough; just barely good enough; satisfactory. If you were to put a letter grade on each, the progression might go something like this: D, D+, C−, C, C+, B−, B, B+, A−, A. It never works out that neatly, of course, since the academic context is different for each assignment—thus a student who does a good job on the book review may turn around and screw up the interview; and this means that his grades would go up and down from week to week, which would be confusing, frustrating, and idiotic all around.

The best system is no system. Give them a mid-term and final grade and nothing else. The mid-term is nothing more than a blunt signal or warning. B means keep doing what you've been doing and you may end up with an A for the course. C means you're not putting as much care into your writing as you should. I never give A's at mid-term. The final grade is the only one that goes into the permanent record (here at least). It usually works out that the A students are the ones with talent (roughly five out of twenty in the nonfiction courses); the B students are the eager-to-learn hard workers who have no professional-level talent but do their best with what they have (roughly ten out of twenty); and the C's and D's are students who've been demoralized by the criticism and have never recovered. The demoralization usually manifests itself in the form of absences. I've never had a student who was unable, intellectually, to do the work.

Believe it or not, no one has ever complained about this system in my six years here. Those students who are obsessively grade-conscious will catch you as you're running down the hall to ask, "How am I doing?" and you can reassure them that they're doing all right or satisfactorily (not fine or well; they'll hold that against you if you give them anything less than an A at the end) and not to give any mind at all to their final grade. Of course there are always three or four students who would flunk the course or get a D if you didn't work with them on the side. This semester I'm working with a pudgy, incredibly mild fellow named Homer Jurgensen, an electrical engineering major who—though I happen to know he has an intelligence quotient of 134—peers at me through his glasses with what appears to be total incomprehension. If it weren't that he initiated our meetings-on-the-side himself I'd consider him almost hopeless as a writing student. He appears not to believe my claim that he has an individual point of view. I'm not sure he even understands that he's a distinct individual. He keeps visiting me between classes, though, bringing papers from his other courses, asking me to go over them with him. Over in Hammerschlag Hall he can apparently grasp any of the complicated mechanical principles they throw at him, but he has a hell of a time understanding what language is all about even though he uses it daily.

· Irrelevant: Homer is agonizingly shy. He happens to sit next to JoAnn Croft, a born-again sophomore who rolls her moped right into the classroom, and I've observed her trying to drag him out of his slide-rule musings while the class is settling down. I don't know whether she's asking him to accept Jesus Christ as his personal tutor or just asking for a date, but Homer turns purple whenever she talks to him. It's hilarious the way he keeps changing seats and she changes with him, but touching too because I suspect that in his heart he's convinced there's nothing there worth bothering about and is more confused than embarrassed. Lucy says it's simpler than all that: He can't stand her. But JoAnn isn't one of those humorless, self-righteous Moonie types; she's bright and funny and a sweet kid. (Homer, I'll give you a passing grade if you let JoAnn take you for a ride on her moped.)

Under ordinary circumstances V. Brown would be working with me between classes too; but I know she'd accuse me of patronizing her, or worse, if I suggested it. (Besides, I'm too chicken.)

Monday, October 16

EXPOSITION I More peer evaluation today. The *Miss Lonelyhearts* reviews were due, but instead of collecting them I asked the students to exchange them with one another—in pairings I had worked out beforehand (the best critics evaluating those whose work probably requires the most extensive constructive criticism). When the assignment-shuffling had been done I wrote the following questions on the board:

1. Does the reviewer have an overall attitude toward the novel? If so, what is that attitude?
2. Paraphrase the reviewer's own ideas (as distinct from West's or Miss Lonelyhearts').
3. Are the reviewer's ideas interesting, somewhat interesting, or uninteresting?
4. Does the reviewer provide examples or illustrations to support his ideas? Are they *all* effective? Which are not?
5. In what way does the reviewer convey the uniqueness of the novel?
6. Does the review have a fundamental flaw? If so, what is it?
7. Is the review entirely logical, line by line? If not, indicate any areas of imprecise or sloppy or fuzzy thinking.
8. In your opinion, does the reviewer control and dominate the material, or is he intimidated by it?
9. Is the review as a whole entertaining or does it read like a routine "student paper" or "English theme" or "book report"?
10. In your (hard-to-please) opinion, is a rewrite called for? Indicate what needs to be done to strengthen the piece, aside from those points you may have already mentioned.

They spent the entire class period answering the

questions in writing, and I collected these directed evaluations, plus the reviews themselves just before the bell rang. Throughout the rest of the week I'll be meeting the students in my office, one at a time, twenty minutes each, and will go over their reviews in detail, showing them what further work needs to be done. This conference system is a great time and labor saver, since you don't have to write your comments all over every page of each of the twenty student papers. It's also an ideal way to slip in praise and encouragement, face to face, with the student in private. There are so many students and so few instructors generally that an undergrad can go through an entire semester without hearing a human-to-human word from a single faculty member. Even if you, as a teacher, turn out to be as awkward on the human-to-human level as I am (there's no way of knowing in advance), you'll find that it doesn't matter during the conferences; the students will glow with pleasure when you praise their work and you yourself will feel slightly drunk—a healthy high that lasts well into evening. And when you meet the class as a whole for the first time afterward you'll notice a relaxation in their bodies and faces, and some of them will look at you as a human being for the first time too.

Except for V. Brown, I fear. When she arrives for her conference she'll be in a defensive mood, to say the least. The situation is complicated by the fact that I think someone has either been doing her homework for her or "helping" her intensively. During the past two weeks her work has jumped from execrable (foolish notions, illogically developed) to good (reasonable and interesting ideas, well written) and the style of composition is drastically different. I'm going to try to devise a method whereby she'll be forced to do her own work and teach herself something—but I'm afraid I'll need help from Jesse Jackson.

Her *Miss Lonelyhearts* review is in such good shape that I don't know what the hell we're going to talk about between 12:00 and 12:20. How can I praise her for work someone else did?

FICTION WORKSHOP We discussed the second version of a student story we had workshopped four weeks ago, and the students were able to see the rewrite principle in action. Too many undergrads come to the workshop firmly convinced that fiction should be created in a free, spontaneous, dreamlike spasm, and resist the notion that what they've written can be improved in any way. You can prepare them for the rewrite trauma by apologizing at an early meeting for the unfortunate and insurmountable eccentricity you have of needing to tamper with their submissions. Or you can frankly admit that in the workshop everyone is going to have to tamper with everyone else's work. At the first sign of outrage you can explain that a submission is a work in progress, not yet cast in bronze, or a puzzle that can be assembled in various ways, with some ways better than others. A mechanism with moving and replaceable parts.

Fortunately, there was a drastic improvement in the second version of Trissy Wolf's story. She had taken to heart our most important critical comments and carried out deletions and compressions and expansions that rendered the new version much stronger as a whole. Things don't always work out so neatly; sometimes the second version is as bad as the first but for different reasons. The main problem in Trissy's original version was "jumping conflict" (as opposed to foreshadowing and slowly rising conflict)—a common flaw in student fiction. Robin falls in love with Lance, "a profound eternal love"; but this profound eternal love vanishes as soon as she learns he's married: "After that her love for him disappeared." Robin, rid of Lance, donates her extraordinarily attractive body to Rex, not in sorrow or rebound but in a sort of what-the-hell way. The overall problem here, excuse me for spelling it out, is that these drastic changes occur too rapidly. Undergrads have a tough time grasping that drama should be dramatic, that simply racing through one development after another is the most undramatic way there is of presenting your socko stuff.

"String it out," you have to say, over and over again.

More on character delineation: On Monday I brought in a volume of stories and simply read aloud the opening paragraphs of each, showing how the writer lets you know right off what sort of protagonist you're going to be dealing with throughout the piece. In many, a simple caricature is sketched out, or at least a clear *type* (worried father, ambitious employee, overhopeful suitor, and so on), and then the writer gently adds the subtle tones and shadows as the story progresses, until finally a three-dimensional character is in focus.

I've mentioned this before, but it bears repeating: It's very helpful to encourage the students to begin thinking in types, even stereotypes, as they sort out the raw elements of their ideas in preparation for writing a story. If you don't encourage this, or something like it, you're likely to find that the characters in their stories are all young, perceptive, sensitive, lonely, and vaguely yearning people who have

81

not done much of anything, are not doing much of anything, and are not even thinking of doing much of anything except vaguely yearning.

(I saw a drawing of a cat the other day with the caption *A cat not thinking of doing anything.*)

You don't insist on relevance, do you?

Tuesday, October 17

EXPOSITION I, OFFICE CONFERENCE DAY Practical suggestions: Don't waste a single moment in chitchat. Have the student sit beside you, slap his paper down on the desk, and read it aloud, interrupting to make whatever professorial comments are necessary and employing as many words of praise as you can ("Smooth transition . . . Interesting choice of verb . . . Strong ending"). Let the student figure out what the problems are; if he can't, point them out in positive, weasel-wordy terms ("I'm wondering if these two sentences wouldn't have an even greater impact if you combined them into one. That way, instead of two relatively weak sentences, you'd have one powerful statement. What you think?").

V. Brown—tall, slender, and stunning in an Accra promenade gown—came in at noon all ready to do battle with the oppressive representative of the forces of capitalism. Such was the manner in which she seemed to regard me. Having read her review four times and finding a handful of rough spots, I proceeded to compliment the freedom fighter on her revolutionary eloquence; but when I dared point out a line or two that might be polished (which would strengthen the piece and thereby devastate the Establishment even more thoroughly) she exploded and I had to change tactics *tout de suite*.

"Let's take a little walk," I said, and led the way up the sloping hall to the chairman's office. I was violating my own rule: Never do anything impulsive in the presence of an undergrad who hankers after biting you; it will be taken as a sign of weakness, which it usually is. Fortunately Dr. Ogilvy was out to lunch.

A debonair turnaround and a graceful glide downslope to the office of Professor Mildred Wilson. After a few minutes in the calming presence of this kindly and remarkably tactful colleague, Comrade Brown allowed as how an adjustment or two in her manifesto might be in order.

Afterward she seemed in a subdued enough mood for me to dare suggest that henceforth she do her own work. She was stunned into silence, which was fine; all I cared about was surviving to see another dawn.

Thursday, October 19

Office conferences are still going on.

I appreciate your interest in my "case." The simplest way to fill you in on the background is to send copies of some old letters to the *Tartan*, which I've just xeroxed for you. Because of these letters, and subsequent pressure on the English department from the faculty review committee and the dean, I was offered a new contract in 1976. Here's the key passage from that committee's official recommendation to the department:

In addition to procedural irregularities, it is clear that a major grievance of Professor Russ concerns itself with the judgement that his work lacks an ethical dimension . . . the Committee is strongly sympathetic with his feelings on this point . . .

Here's the letter to the *Tartan* that kicked things off, followed by the chairman's response, followed by my response to his:

November 18, 1975

Editor: I am an associate professor of English who has been told recently by the department Chairman that I had better seek employment elsewhere because it is certain I will be denied tenure at Carnegie-Mellon University. I am writing this letter to bring to your attention the reasons why, according to Dr. McMasters, my contract will not be renewed.

Dr. McMasters said that while I am considered to be "a tough teacher" who "sets high standards of excellence," whose colleagues "respect your work, your teaching, your professionalism," still it is the opinion of the department's Promotions & Tenure Committee that I am "not yet a novelist" (despite having published three novels, with a fourth to come out next year). Dr. McMasters went on to mention "a departmental concern that much of your work deals with the military," and that there is "an absence of political, social or moral judgement in your publications—a lack of ethical dimension." Finally, Dr. McMasters said that I had "failed to provide energetic, programmatic leadership."

It's not the firing itself that I am protesting, but rather the reasons given for it. It's clear that my publications were given

84

only cursory examination by the Committee; otherwise the very odd departmental concerns mentioned by the Chairman could not have arisen. What bothers me most, however, is the implication that a writer is expected to restrict himself to an ethical framework. (It so happens that I do, if anyone on the Committee had taken the trouble to check—but that's beside the point.) It truly astonishes me that professors of English, supposedly sensitive to any threat on academic freedom, could allow such a wretched implication to go unchallenged.

As far as the "failure to provide energetic, programmatic leadership" is concerned: I was under the impression that I was hired to teach and publish. Since Professor Florian Beeler happens to be the efficient director of the Creative Writing staff, I can only wonder what sort of leadership was expected of me, and more than that, wonder why all this wasn't mentioned long ago so that I might shape up instead of having to ship out.

Once again let me say that it's not the firing I'm protesting but the inept deliberations of my concerned colleagues.

Martin Russ,
English Department

November 25, 1975

Editor: Since Professor Russ has used the columns of the *Tartan* to lodge a complaint against the promotions committee of the English department, perhaps a reply in the same columns is in order. Professor Russ' account of my report to him about the grounds of the committee's judgements is accurate. I did indeed tell him that he was regarded as "a tough teacher," who set "high standards of excellence," one whom his colleagues respected for his writing, his teaching, his professionalism. And I reported that there were those in our committee who had reservations about his competence as a novelist, about the narrowness of his vein of reportorial excellence, about the "lack of ethical dimension" in his accounts of Korea, and Tarawa.

Professor Russ is mistaken, I think, in judging that his "publications were given only cursory examination by the committee," though the committee is large and may have contained members who had not sufficiently reviewed Professor Russ' work. The fact remains, however, that the judgements I reported to him were both made and thoughtfully canvassed by members of the committee.

I think I understand these judgements, though I do not weigh them equally. I have read almost all that Professor Russ has published in book form; I have read many of his reviews, articles, and scripts; I have read his current novel in two of its drafts. And I am left with this personal assessment: that Professor Russ' very real gifts as a writer find their best expression at present in the reportorial or journalistic rather than the fictional, and that his gifts have shown themselves primarily in military accounts.

That these accounts have an ethical base I agree with Professor Russ; but since it receives little verbalization, little development or elaboration, I understand the dismay of the critics who ask of him more, much more, than they find. What's involved here is not a violation of academic freedom, nor is it accurate to infer that the committee expected "a writer to restrict himself to an ethical framework." The committee members were not urging a framework of any kind; they were not positing an approved ethical vision. They *were* expressing a sense of significant privation.

As for the "failure to provide energetic . . . leadership," it is true that several members of the committee felt strongly about this. It is also true that Professor Russ did not provide much leadership. And it is finally true that the department failed adequately to communicate to Professor Russ its need, the sense of which only emerged after Professor Sims left us for another academic post.

Martin, Martin, we who care about communication have communicated too little too late. The reason you're being let go is not that you're not a very good teacher, nor that you're not a far better than ordinary writer. The reasons are three: that as its creative writing commitment grows, the department needs an established writer of fiction, it needs energetic leadership, and it must spend its few tenure slots with a prudence verging on the parsimonious. Tenure was the basic issue in the committee's

86

extended deliberations about you. In the last analysis it was tenure that made you a casualty. I'm sorry.

John McMasters
Chairman, English Dept.

February 10, 1976

Editor: While I appreciate the gentlemanly manner with which Dr. McMasters responded to my letter of November 18, I wish to point out to those who are interested that he sidesteps a vital issue: that the Promotions & Tenure Committee of the English Department, in its deliberations over the question of my tenure, considered the moral dimension of my published work to be relevant. It seems only too obvious that a writer's moral stance should not be used as a tenure yardstick: further, that if it *is* used, its degree of verbalization, development and elaboration should not be prescribed or restricted by a committee. I am frankly astonished at the collective wrongheadedness of the P & T Committee in considering as a basis for denying tenure the issue of a writer's ethics and moral judgement.

While I'm willing to acknowledge that I'm indeed a minor writer it nevertheless strikes me as unfortunate that a committee of English professors, none of whom have ever published a novel—and very little else on the open market—would presume to question the competence of a colleague whose novels have not only been published but widely reviewed. Notice that I didn't say "question the artistic value"; I said question the competence—for that is the word Dr. McMasters used in his letter of November 25.

Martin Russ
English Dept.

Incidentally, I'm thinking of writing another letter to the *Tartan* and of taking my case once again to the faculty review committee; the only trouble is that I can't figure out precisely what my complaint is!

Friday, October 20

Students learn more if they write more. In too many workshops, the instructor requires only twenty pages or so by the end of the semester. Such a light page requirement indirectly encourages the student to have an attitude of preciousness toward his work. Next year, if there is a next year, I'm going to double the page requirement. I've been lazy about this.

In many ways the teaching of writing is the easiest kind, since the students are constantly bringing stuff to you that they need a lot of help with. This is to say, there are always a great many remarks that obviously need to be made about each paper, and most any clear-thinking adult can make them. The same cannot be said with regard to history courses or physics courses or acting courses or most other kinds of courses. The only disadvantage is that a writing teacher has to do an extraordinary amount of detailed reading, and any writing teacher who reaches middle age without wearing glasses wears contact lenses. "I love your eyes," Lucy said awhile back. "All four of them."

As I mentioned earlier, my students have to write detailed evaluations of the story or stories to be discussed on a particular day. Even the writers themselves have to do it. I also assign them specific elements of the stories to talk about in class: for example, one student will be ready to discuss the characterizations, another the plotting, another the setting, another the theme, another the style or approach or point of view. If you decide to follow this system, make sure to collect the written evaluations at the beginning of class; otherwise most of the students will write them *during* class, after they have discerned the consensus opinion—and most of them will be so tentative as to be almost noncommittal. Along about the third week it's a good idea to chew them out for their lack of commitment. Warn them that they're going to read their evaluations aloud at the next meeting. This will force them or at least strongly encourage them to take a stand and come to grips with the stories in a critical way.

The over-thirty characters in many undergrad stories are pompous, insensitive, vulgar, unimaginative, crassly materialistic, hypocritical, self-deluding, stupid, and often totally wrongheaded about everything. You must try to convince them of the naïveté of such sweeping indictments. It isn't hard—most quickly recognize the crudeness of such characterizations and know that damn few folks, if any, behave like this. One of the ways you justify yourself as a teacher of talentless students is to tell yourself that at least you're teaching them a little something about the nature of middle-aged man—that while he may be a humble ass, a pompous ass, a sanctimonious ass, a colossal ass, or an insignificant ass, at least there are various *kinds* of asses. A small accomplishment, to be sure, but something.

—Freshman and sophomores and many juniors are as a rule maddeningly passive, doing only what is expected of them, rarely questioning you or any other part of the system, wanting nothing so much as to get their academic degree and take wing in the World. This is perfectly natural, of course, but it's particularly bothersome to a fiction workshop teacher because it means that the protagonists in their stories are passive too. I suggest that you show them that almost all of the great stories are built around an active struggle of some kind. You have to be cautious, though, because undergrads generally do not admire the great fiction of the past and resist being asked to do so. (An English major may be willing to treat Henry James and Proust and Melville respectfully in his literature classes and admire them in an academic sort of way, but in the workshop setting you're dealing with emotional preferences, and most undergrads prefer the worst of Barthelme to the best of Conrad, the worst of Pynchon to the best of Mann.) Most of the fiction they truly admire has to do with passive people in static situations, stories in which style and form are nearly everything. Such fiction is usually tiresomely experimental, "innovative" and texture-obsessed, reeking with academic avant-gardyness. The concern with style and form often adds up to a kind of stylish formlessness—a series of noncommittal descriptions of trivial details in nondeveloping situations, sometimes executed with remarkable ingenuity and verbal boldness. This is a fad or fashion that will pass, for the fiction-needing masses want, at bottom, the same kind of tale told around the campfire by the earliest yarn-spinners.

Monday, October 23

In answer to your friendly question: I'm feeling fine! Lucy keeps asking when I'm going to throw my can of Iron

City at the wall and start bellowing. The reason I'm feeling fine is that I think I can beat them on this, again, and I like a good fight.

Now, about tenure. You can identify the instructors and assistant professors of English (that is, the untenured members of the department) by their hunted haunted harried look, for all of them are painfully aware that the most important thing in their lives right now is to publish before they perish. Accordingly, they spend a good part of their time desperately thrashing about in some tiny corner of scholarship that they hope hasn't already been picked clean by the instructors and assistant professors who've gone before, striving to perform Promethean tasks in Procrustean beds. Sometimes they'll go to ludicrous and almost incredible lengths to carve out their own little niches—for instance, the instructor presently collecting acronyms, starting with the one for Alcoholics Anonymous and the one for Automobile Association of America; all this for a "Study in Communication-Convenience Controls." Or the instructor collecting graffiti in the toilets of private colleges and universities in New England (with the aid of a graduate student who takes care of the Hers side of things) for "A Study in Language Differences in Various Eliminatory Pastimes." Both studies presumably are to be submitted to the Carnegie-Mellon University Press for inclusion in its consistently unread Developing Language Series.

I have the impression, nevertheless, that it is the untenured in most English departments who are the most effective *teachers*. This is largely due to the anxiety arising from job insecurity, which forces them to work at full capacity. The most effective motivator for any teacher is fear. (The knowledge that your students expect to get their

91

money's worth in every class is scary enough.) Tenure, it seems to me, neutralizes this fear and is therefore the enemy of good teaching. It was invented, so I understand, to protect academic freedom; but the freedom it protects, more often than not, is the freedom to teach poorly. And I'm wondering if professors really need more freedom than anyone else. How many nontenured professors were actually fired for speaking out against our involvement in Vietnam? Damn few, I think. Where are all these professors who would lose their jobs were it not for the safeguard of tenure? There aren't any at Carnegie-Mellon. Only the rarest professor has any startlingly new and unsettling ideas anyway, and most of your shocking professors work at Harvard, Berkeley, Stanford, Chicago, and three or four other places where they're not likely to get thrown out.

The tenured professor is never forced to justify his classroom work to his students, and can go on year after year in a take-it-or-leave-it way in which arrogance overrides the kind of teaching that has to do with helping, sharing, giving. I'm not suggesting that all tenured professors are arrogant and lazy; there are at least three in this department (Stanley Urbanic, Mildred Wilson, Walter Kravanja) who have retained their personal fascination with their specialties and share it every day with their students.

Here's a passage I culled from a graduate student's novel-in-progress: "Tenure . . . is an administratively conferred state of being in which a faculty member, having proven himself in an apprenticeship to have no inclination to cause any trouble at all, is given the security to cause the trouble that everyone knows he never will . . . Anyone with tenure must have clearly demonstrated no need for its protection." *

Rather than guaranteeing a professor his job security until he's sixty-five, it would make more sense to keep renewing his contract only as long as he continues to fulfill his duties competently. A new teacher should be given a one-year contract, and then, assuming he does well, a two- or three-year contract, and then finally a series of five-year contracts.

Now, about John McMasters. He was axed for being unable to come up with a coherent departmental goal to satisfy the money-obsessed provosts and President Moore. It seems to me that Alan Ogilvy was hired after convincing the administration he'll be able to devise a goal that will attract grant money from government, industry, and private angels. I thought Dr. McMasters was a terrific chairman, but that goes to show how little I know. I liked his decisive manner, among other things. Some of the colleagues are still grumbling about how he failed to consult the various committees about this and that, for failing to convoke the interminable and ludicrously indecisive meetings that Dr. Ogilvy is already showing himself partial to. I also liked him personally because he was witty in a nonacademic way, because he teased me from time to time, because he took the trouble to read two wretched versions of my novel and made helpful comments. Most of all I liked him because he had the nerve to hire an unknown writer with hardly any teaching experience and no degree. Why he gave me the exalted title of associate

* "Scolly's Law," by Scarff Downing.

professor I don't know (some of the tenured members were very upset about this, I learned later), but needless to say *I* didn't question it. Before he left I sent him a sentimental note thanking him for sticking his neck out so far. If he hadn't done so I'd probably be working as a prison guard in Huntingdon right now.

I'm not a fan of Alan Ogilvy's, although it's really too early to pass judgment. I'll do so anyway. He was introduced to us by Dean Atterbury as "a nationally prominent rhetorician who brings with him a strong research interest in the cognitive processes involved in writing," and when I hear the word rhetorician I unholster my Luger. Already he's introducing policies that seem cockeyed to me. For example, he wants each member of the department to turn in every month a detailed account of his professional activities. Here's the list he passed out at the first meeting, each item of which we are to account for every month:

1. Publications
2. Funded research
3. Other professional activities (papers, lectures, consultations, conferences, etc.)
4. Work in progress
5. Supervision of graduate students
6. Service (committees, civic service, etc.)
7. Other (instructional innovations, honors and awards, etc.)

Notice something amazing: There's nothing on the list about teaching, at least not the teaching of undergraduates, which is what we spend most of our time doing.

Here's a cranky memo I dashed off about the list:

Dear Alan: You asked us to respond to the Monthly Activities Form you handed out.

It curls my toes.

I consider myself a teacher who writes on the side for his own pleasure. Whatever research and work-in-progress I happen to be into is a private matter. Not secret or confidential, just private as opposed to public. I can't imagine a so-called creative writer worth his salt who writes for academic colleagues or for future students.

Whatever salary increases I get should be based, it seems to me, largely on the rate of inflation and the degree to which students feel I have helped them improve their writing . . .

The next day Dr. Ogilvy said he intended to sit down with me and discuss the memo, but I haven't heard from him since and don't expect to—any more than I expect him to find out what the committee meant by saying collectively that my administrative input leaves something to be desired. That is the administrator's way: do nothing until you're forced to do something, and then do as little of it as possible.

At the second English faculty meeting Dr. Ogilvy announced a drastic new departmental commitment—a document design program, in which students will be trained to write government contracts and other official documents, including instruction manuals. Not a bad idea, in view of Secretary Califano's revelations about the appalling bureaucratic gobbledygook that passes for communication in government offices. I've seen a few pages of the original grant-seeking proposal, however, and it is in itself almost a parody of the kind of academic-bureaucratic writing that English professors are supposed to be holding the line against. Notice with what off-putting solemnity these common-sense (and common-knowledge) principles are stated in this typical excerpt:

1. . . . We have already discussed the differences in audience constraints for the two versions. Cultural factors that should be considered are discussed in Section D below. Contextual constraints include the fact that the contract will be a preprinted form. This means it must have sufficient flexibility to cover many possible circumstances . . . When there are both sets of operators and sets of tasks, the organization of tasks by persons will make it easier for people to understand what they must do. This principle comes from the research of Hindeman *et al.* at Carnegie-Mellon University . . .
2. Group ideas logically facilitate recall.
3. A corollary of the second principle is that presenting ideas in logical order facilitates recall.
4. Limiting each paragraph to one main idea facilitates recall. Again, this is a principle from institutional research . . .

President Carter should establish a new Cabinet post—Secretary of Language; or at least found an Academy like the one in France. Edwin Newman could do the job. I don't know if you're acquainted with his work; he's one of the blazing archangels of our language. Not an effete word-snob or "rhetorician" or "linguistics analyst," but simply a man committed to a probably hopeless battle against pretension, obscurity, emotional and intellectual mendacity, and plain sloppiness in speech and writing. During his appearance on the Cavett show, which I taped, he quoted from an environmental-impact report from the administrative files of San José State:

Traffic congestion will result from vehicular trip-generation associated with stadium usage. Expansion of the stadium will exacerbate neighborhood nuisance-impacts by pushing on-street parking further into the residential area.

As Newman went on to say, the language here suggests that something extremely difficult to understand is taking place, and that if one can convey that very impression, one's job is likely to be safe, as well as one's "funding." The writer wanted to hide the fact that all he had to say was "If you make the stadium bigger there'll be more traffic."

This kind of jargon-polluted writing is being required of more and more students around the country, and I was appalled to learn at our meeting that it will now be required of Carnegie-Mellon students as well.

To say that I've spent the past seven years teaching students in nonfiction classes to write simply and clearly is no boast at all, since that's what instructors in English are supposed to do. Unfortunately, very few of them do so. The situation is further complicated by the fact that many professors in other departments require papers written in the academic-bureaucratic style. Semester by semester my students are increasingly confused: Professor Russ is demanding one style of writing while many of his colleagues demand another. Don't think I'm trying to picture myself as Leonidas at Thermopylae—but I *am* one of the Three Hundred. And so are Stanley Urbanic, Mildred Wilson, and Walter Kravanja.

It's easy to demonstrate that anything said in academic-bureaucratic language can be said more efficiently and effectively if it's said simply and clearly. No concept or idea is so complicated and subtle and complex that it can't be conveyed in a series of simple, direct sentences. (It's true that you may need a great many such sentences in a row.) By way of sermonette I assure the students that there isn't a single boss out in the jargon-corrupted World who will be anything but delighted to discover an employee who can write simply and clearly, and that such an employee stands a better chance at promotion than his co-workers, all else being equal. I wish I believed that.

Two practical suggestions:

1. In several successive classes, bring in a few short paragraphs written in the New Dialect and ask the students to translate. I'll send you examples from my vast collection on request.

2. Many students have been writing in the academic-bureaucratic style for so long that they find it almost impossible to break the habit. "But I can't figure out any other way to say it," is a complaint you often hear. Suggest to the student that he simply blurt it out conversationally without stopping to think about it. Nine times out of ten he'll say it in a simpler, clearer, and more graceful way than what's down on paper.

Isn't there a foundation somewhere willing to lay a grant on an English department whose goal is to train students to write simply and clearly? On the other hand, is there an English department even capable of doing so? *This* English department seems interested only in recruiting more professors who themselves write in the New Dialect.

Here's a typical quote from the *curriculum vita* of a current candidate for appointment:

Current Research Interests: Discourse analysis (particularly the interaction of discourse phenomena with sentence-level syntax);

Linguistic typology and language universals (particularly the search for statistical correlations between basic constituent order and sets of transformations in the grammars of individual languages).

Dissertation: "An Explanation of the Distribution of Basic Constituent Orders": A statistical analysis of the frequency of the logically possible basic constituent orders is presented and explained in terms of the interaction of three independently motivated grammatical principles.

Another piece of evidence to support my theory that higher education is too important to be left in the hands of professors.

FICTION WORKSHOP May I suggest that you encourage your students to Think Gross? The undergraduate imagination is awfully timid, and writing students in particular need to be goosed in the fundament. Thinking Gross simply means thinking in terms of the unusual, exploring the wildest possibilities for your characters and plot and setting. Dürrenmatt is right in saying a story is incomplete until it has taken its worst possible turn. By the final draft the student will have toned everything down and balanced it all out to the best of his ability, so there's no harm in "going too far" in the first draft. Besides, it's fun. As Terence O'Haggarty said the other day, "Can't a writer have some fun?" Better to start the torturous rewriting process with too much material than too little. I once heard a stage director say that he prefers rehearsing with people who overact because it's so much easier to pare off excess fat than to try to graft on muscle.

While a tale about a middle-aged woman's lust for a fourteen-year-old boy is relatively unusual (the premise of Abigail Boretsky's story for tomorrow), a tale about a middle-aged virgin's lust for a fourteen-year-old boy who turns out to be a gigolo is *highly* unusual, and I'm going to encourage Abigail to explore that possibility tomorrow. She will probably be disgusted or at least offended, but I think she'll recognize that such a possibility is inherent in the material (no grafting-on necessary) and that it could provide the emotional and dramatic impact the story in its present form lacks. All this is sheer gimmickry on my part, to be sure, but undergrads need to learn that most of the great plays, films, and novels have some variety of gimmick at the core—by which I mean simply an unusual premise. It's important for them to know that if they must write a story about a campus love affair (and many must), it *must* have some fresh twist or at least be told from a new angle.

"You're talking about commercial fiction," said Monci Jo Nickerson, frowning.

"That too. And not only fiction. Anything you want to sell."

"Sell?" she said, her face puckering up.

"Anything you want to publish, then."

"Must have a *gimmick?*" said Bud Carr, who brings out the worst in me. Every time I see him I wish to flatten his "Cat" with a pig bladder.

"All right. Let's say you want to sell a collection of celebrity portraits. Editors are going to want to know what the gimmick is. Celebrities sitting in chairs looking at the camera? Yes, but what's the gimmick? No gimmick? No sale . . . Ah, but if your celebrities happen to be sitting on their toilet seats, and the title of your collection is *Going to Pot,* then—"

"That is gross," said Trissy Wolf.

"Gross Thinking will win the day!"

"What does this have to do with literature?" asked Bud Carr.

"That is a very good question. Don't ask it again."

Wednesday, October 25

A note from Professor Joe Hoffnitz of the computer science department, who just heard about the firing. "The trouble is probably that you aren't one of the boys," it says in part. I'd hate to think that's all it boils down to. He offered to help in any way possible. I may go to him for advice, although at the moment I don't know what advice to seek.

The only other faculty member who has said a word about the firing is Yves Mirandelle, French professor, who happens to be the only colleague I've made a move toward in my six years here. Our relationship, such as it is, is based on a mutual nostalgia for Vietnam. For the last two years we've shared the pipedream of going back there together to gather material for a book. That he's a novelist, a wounded war veteran, and a frantically doting father means something to me. He had some bad luck during the pre–Dien Bien Phu fighting and bears all sorts of psychic scars; but the thing that attracts me most is his naïve willingness to reveal himself at all times. To talk with him for one hour is to know everything about him, so unlike the English professors, who never reveal anything. He's very disorganized, racing hither and thither, with agitation marks flying from his crazy hair as he tries to cope. A galloping shambles of a man, but a good teacher (I audited two of his courses and learned much more than I expected to). Anyway, I got a note from him too, saying he had written a letter of protest to Dean Atterbury but that "the face he made when we discussed it in the hall indicated that there's little hope of reversal." (The note is signed, "Your friend in hopes and dreams.")

That's it, as far as faculty support is concerned.

The chairman has called a departmental meeting for Thursday, an unusual move, "to continue the discussion of the document design program." Some of the colleagues are unhappy about the proposal, but for the wrong reasons.

Yesterday I was sitting in my office when I heard a loud knock and in stalked Wallace M. Sample, Jr., a sophomore from the Expo class. Hails from New Hampshire. Laconic. Today he set some kind of record for silence. There was something very much on his mind but he couldn't get it out, and at one point in the twenty-five-minute "conference" he sat wordless for five minutes, staring at me while I stared back pretending to be calm, which I never am under any circumstances. There was no question that it was a contest of some sort, if not an outright battle of wills.

"Aren't you going to say anything?" he finally asked.

"No," I said—amiably, sadistically.

Wallace never did find words to tell me what was bothering him, but I think I know. I had come on too strong in Friday's class, was too sure of myself, too brazenly self-confident, a regular Mr. Smartypants Know-it-all, and Wallace wanted to let me know I don't deserve such a lofty opinion of myself. If this interpretation seems far-fetched I can only assure you I've had many similar experiences with undergrads who, without realizing it consciously, decide that it's the instructor himself rather than his methods and course material they despise. My guess is that Wallace has reached the crisis point in his natural resistance to criticism and has become acutely anxious over my incessant demand that he commit himself in writing to a definite personal opinion about *something*. I was hoping that his unexpected visit would turn out to be an occasion of pedagogy instead of an occasion of sadism. If he had been able to tell me how furious he was, I would have applauded him for taking a definite stand and making an interpretive statement—as I applauded the student years ago who gave a speech on the worthlessness of my course.

I can't apologize for being so breezily self-assured in Friday's class (almost any instructor who knows his subject and has taught it for several years is sure of himself); but I will admit to making a mistake in public relations. Human nature is such that we tend to resent anyone who gives the impression of cockiness, even if the cockiness is warranted; and since the emotions of most undergrads are very close to the surface, often dominating the intellect, the wise instructor will try to comport himself in a modest if not humble manner. He'll say, "Let's try it out this way and see what you-all think about it," instead of, "Now *this* is the way it should be done."

FICTION WORKSHOP The students were in an unusually friendly mood today after I read aloud Thurber's A *Couple of Hamburgers*; it seemed to turn them jolly en masse. It's a useful piece for illustrating the Show-Don't-Tell principle. The students agreed that it would've weakened the story had Thurber intruded with unnecessary explanations (exposition). It's useful too for illustrating simple characterization and the gradual build-up of tension. A *Couple of Hamburgers* is a battle-of-the-sexes story, the reader witnessing a low-keyed engagement of that battle. The low-key aspect is convenient for classroom purposes; there's nothing clever or flashy about the story that might intimidate the undergrads.

Lucy has another theory as to why they were so animated today—I wore my new glasses for the first time. Not so much the appearance of the new pair as the absence of the old—small, round, wire-rimmed, which she called "your genocide specials."

Friday, October 27

"Where do you think we'll be a year from now?" asked Lucy this morning.

I had a vision of the Russ family in residence behind the Midas Muffler billboard overlooking Exit 12 of the Pennsylvania Turnpike, but said I wouldn't be surprised to find us in the Napa Valley. A certain chill in the bowels this morning, worrying over the future for the first time. Never look ahead, never look behind, and never look around.

Back to business. Every few semesters you'll find yourself stuck in a classroom with students who seem so collectively bent on preserving their anonymity that it seems you can't teach them a damn thing. In my thirteen semesters here I've had to deal with this situation twice, and both times it was probably my fault entirely: I was too bumptiously obnoxious, didn't let them do enough talking (because those who talked talked inanely), and dominated them in a way that drove them even further into their natural undergrad timidity. Desperately drastic methods were forced on me both times.

In the first instance I devoted an entire classroom period to teaching them the rudiments of poker, then sent them to see and review *The Cincinnati Kid*. This was risky only because it smacked of the kind of "good guy" exercise that students despise. The other situation was far riskier, but I was lucky there too and the result was startling. I delivered, very formally, a lecture purporting to shoot down the theory of evolution, which is not that difficult to do given the contradictory if not downright dubious evidence; but when you discuss the theory with most people you're into emotion rather than reason. It's the only theory we have, after all (not counting that other one), and very few scientists, let alone laymen, are ready to allow it to be called into question. I had instructed the students to take notes and then write a review of the lecture. As I had expected, most of them were vibrating with shock and chagrin over finding themselves in the presence of a professor who seemed to profess that an all-powerful supernatural Creator had conceived, designed, executed, and is now sustaining the universe and who knows what all. Such was the implication of the lecture, but you can be damn sure I didn't come right out and say so directly. Instead I merely claimed that the gap between animals and man had not been bridged by "missing links" and that the fossil evidence reveals none of the transitional stages that one would expect to find in abundance. After reading their hot-headed reviews two days later—most of which had invisible exclamation marks of outrage at the end of every sentence—I teased them at the next meeting and was able to make them laugh at themselves. (One of the reviews was titled *Professor Goes Ape: Students Anxiously Await Return of Writing Teacher*, but this was the only one with any suggestion of humor.) I teased them for automatically overreacting to a perfectly harmless, shallowly researched, ineptly presented fifty-minute monologue. I teased them for the shrill and stuffy language they had used in their reviews and said that with one exception all they had done was to write an ineffectual critique of an ineffectual lecturer. I teased them for allowing their emotions to overcome their intellect and said they had used a 155-mm artillery piece to blast a gopher. I insisted that a critic should remain coldly observant in a snakelike sort of way, and that when he strikes it should be done with concentrated control, never exerting more force than necessary. And then I congratulated them for taking a definite stand in their reviews, for letting their individuality as writers show itself for the first time, and told them I was right proud of them. They beamed!

—Grab every opportunity to give the individual student a verbal pat on the back, but expect no reassurance in return. Undergrads aren't much into reassurance, even if you should turn out to be a brilliant Visiting Writer. Whatever compliments you get will come indirectly, and after it's all over, often in the form of a half-insult ("You sure shook me up, man.").

EXPOSITION 1 A sort of wrap-up lecture today about reviewers and reviewing, with the following underlying

106

theme: you can't call yourself an interpretive writer unless you're willing to take a stand, expose your biases and prejudices, and make moral judgments right and left. I managed to slip in some indirectly self-serving remarks about how we all resent anyone with strong opinions, yet how glad we are to have folks like John Simon around to jar us into the kind of meditation that helps us figure out where we stand on this or that issue. Further remarks on how fine it is to live in a society where a brilliant son of a bitch like Simon can flail about viciously and teach us a little something at the same time.

"Boldly take your stand," said the inspired preacher. "Support it plausibly and let the chips fall where they may. By our opinions we define ourselves." (Let us pray.)

At that point I found myself quoting Max Reger's put-down of a certain critic of his work: "I am sitting in the smallest room of my house. I have your review in front of me. Soon it will be behind me." The students did not laugh. They did not even groan. They did not do anything at all, so I hurried on to the next item on the agenda, a quote from John Crowe Ransom: "A professional critic is someone who, in dealing with a work of art, creates a little work of art in its honor."

You can point out that taking a strong stand on an issue, then watching everyone get flustered, is lots of fun in a perverse sort of way. The sentiment may be a trifle juvenile, but you need to use every possible method to get them to commit themselves in their writing. Do you happen to recall Roger Sale's review of *Slapstick* in the *New York Times?* * A mean-spirited piece of work it is,

* *New York Times*, October 3, 1976.

though well-written and entertaining. The students usually admire the way Sale sticks his neck out, even though they don't like what he says. His review provoked so many angry letters (including one from me) that he was called on to respond in a later issue. All this is fun to trace in class, which is why I'm mentioning it. In the past two or three semesters I've managed to work this into a lecture about the Duties and Responsibilities of the Reviewer, the purpose being to get the students to formulate their own definition of what a reviewer should do. (*Should* is a highly provocative word to use in the presence of undergrads—along with *must* and *can't*—but there are times when it's necessary.)

I find myself unable to resist quoting my own letter to the editor. (Perhaps you're unaware that one of the common sneers against English professors is that, in their desperation for tenure or reappointment, they sometimes cite—under publications—any letters-to-the-editor they've been able to get printed.)

Editor: Roger Sale remarks that "nothing could be easier, surely," than for Kurt Vonnegut to have written *Slapstick, or Lonesome No More!* and goes on to point out that Thomas Pynchon and Joseph Heller "took seven and twelve years trying to get *Gravity's Rainbow* and *Something Happened* right." Leaving aside the questionable assumption that any book can be easily written, I'd like to point out that Sale equates the prolific with the second-rate, which is nonsense. He also remarks, gratuitously, that "Vonnegut is now getting almost as rich as the Rosewaters and the Swains," the implication being that a novelist who is popular and therefore rich must also be second-rate.

"It takes no more than a few idle hours to turn the pages of *Slapstick*," he grumbles. "It takes stamina, determination and a crazy intelligence to read Pynchon's two enormous novels." True; but for some of us, a novel requiring determination and stamina to get through is a novel we'll not bother to finish. (A few of us might even admit in a moment of weakness that we read novels for pleasure.) Sale's attitude toward fiction is that of the undergraduate: Kafka is obviously more "significant" than Hemingway because his stuff is difficult—and besides he was obscure and poor.

The students, incidentally, didn't know I wrote that letter (none had seen it in the *Times* and when I read it aloud to them I gave it a made-up signature). I think it's a mistake for a writing teacher to use *anything* of his own in an undergrad course unless he hides the fact. The negatively oriented students, not to mention your Strident, will accuse you of arrogance or egotism in presuming to hold your own stuff up as the way it ought to be done—even if you've only said that it's one way it can be done. Professor Gretchen Wylie, who teaches one of the other workshops, reads her own stuff from time to time and I've heard unkind and unfair remarks about it, despite the fact that she's a good writer who is in no way showing off but merely using a handy illustration of this principle or that.

Velma put on an extraordinary display in today's class. With ten minutes to go, I asked the students to answer two questions in writing:

1. What is unique, or at least unusual, about your character-personality-psyche? (In other words, in what way are you a distinct individual? Describe that individuality.)
2. What are you particularly good at, in comparison with most of your peers? (In other words, describe any expertise you have.)

This exercise is one of several I use to encourage students to try to see themselves as individuals with special attitudes and opinions worth writing about; but the questions themselves are for many undergrads quite threatening, and they pushed Velma right over the edge.

"These are stupid questions," she said.

Melissa Harkness, the dominating member of the class (skeptical about many of my theories but intelligently so) turned on her instantly. "What the hell's stupid about them?" she asked, and was just launching a verbal attack when I intervened in the usual maddeningly bland way.

"Velma may be right about that, but let's see what you-all can do with the questions anyway."

The students lowered their heads and began struggling over the exercise. It was plain that most of them hadn't thought about these things, and were not enjoying having to think about them now. Yet I sensed no hostility or even resentment—aside from Velma's—and sat there hoping everyone would recognize that the abrupt assignment fit neatly into the interpretive writing theme of the course itself, and that it's easier to write interpretively if you know where you stand in relation not to the cosmos but the consensus.

Just before the bell rang I said I had no intention of collecting their answers, "since it's no one's business but your own." Velma snarled aloud, ripped her paper into little pieces, threw them every which way, and stalked out.

—You must be extremely careful about everything you say in the presence of a black student. I saw Velma's body snap into a terrible rigidity a few weeks ago when I happened to use the phrase "black humor" in the sense of gallows humor, and there's no doubt that she was poised to slap the Racist label on me. If you think I'm exaggerating in all this, you'll have to learn for yourself that black undergrads are, generally, so sensitive that almost anything you say having to do with minorities is likely to be taken as racist.

Here's the mid-term exam for Exposition I in case you're interested:

1. What, in your opinion, has the instructor been trying to teach (the central concepts, that is)?

   NOTE: The question is *not* "What have you learned so far?"

2. Write down a commonplace idea, then make a unique or startling or surprising interpretation of that idea. (Your interpretive statement must be logical and plausible.)

3. Write down a principle or an abstract concept ("Water seeks its own level," "It's better to give than to receive"), then provide a specific example of it *in action* in your own life.

4. What mid-term grade do you think you deserve, and why?

Monday, October 30

Over the weekend I mailed applications to Virginia Tech, M.I.T., Bennington, and Skidmore. Bennington is the only one that seems wrong, even though the ad seems to say they're looking for someone of my stripe. Such a tiny student body, though. Such an art-obsessed place. And me such a philistine. Bennington, they tell me, is one of those total-involvement joints, teachers and students all over each other constantly; I doubt if I could survive a month in that kind of hothouse atmosphere. For one thing, I'd have to spend a lot of time discussing Literature, which I despise. For another, there'd be no way to escape the dreaded Literature professors; in a place like Bennington everybody's "working closely with" everybody else, and if you're not team-teaching a course in Tibetan Spacecakes you're involved in whipping up a batch of committed, caring, carob-covered counterculture cupcakes for the mess hall.

I don't yet understand the source of my antipathy toward Literature professors. The pervasive air of smugness has something to do with it. I ran across an appallingly presumptuous statement the other day by Professor Milo Todorvich that conveys that smugness marvelously, although he wasn't talking about Literature professors specifically:

> Being *the* developers of new knowledge as well as *the* depository of the old, college and university faculties have been and still are the *only* available arbiters in matters of knowledge and of dissemination of knowledge. (Italics mine.)

I've paid some attention to the publications of my colleagues (particularly during the two years I served on the promotions and tenure commiteee) and have the impression that they are responsible for a staggering quantity of inconsequentia. English professors are always turning out extraneous "textbooks" (free copies arrive in my mailbox every week; I've examined literally hundreds of them) or else are collecting other people's writing and publishing them as anthologies. My favorite local example—if you'll allow me a moment of rottenness—is something "edited by" two of our tenured battleships, Luther Yerkes and B. T. Ornduff, and proudly displayed behind glass in the departmental office. It's called *Affirmations of the Human Spirit: Readings in Excellence*, and is little more than excerpts from the *Aeneid*, *The Divine Comedy*, and *Paradise Lost* with a one-paragraph introduction to each. Many of the local professor-products are patched together with the primary goal of preserving their authors from perishing in the publish-or-perish sense, or else for some low-wattage pedantic reason; in any case, they tend to shorten the lives of those forced to do "readings in" them. Boredom, like speed, kills.

I detest the idea of Organized Literature and the kind of artificial force-feeding that goes on in some classrooms. A lot of people don't *want* to like D. H. Lawrence or Henry James and I for one will ignore them to the grave. Literature is a private affair, to be indulged in privately, more like a vice than a study. In this private affair you have brief relationships with the author and his characters; if you don't enjoy their company you needn't return to the party.

I was just thinking of the time twenty-five years ago when Sgt. Gonzales flipped a thin paperback across the trench saying he had enjoyed it, and after I read it I passed it along to Cpl. McGrath with the same comment; it was called *Catcher in the Rye* and written by a civilian we'd never heard of. How I'd resent being "assigned" *Wild Strawberries* (a current project in the "film arts" course nearby) and forced to listen to a passionless professor explain what Bergman was trying to do and how he went about doing it. How much better to slouch into a theater on your own and let Bergman himself show you everything he wants you to know about dreams, love, growing old, dying—all in two hours—and not have to talk about it afterward. For most people it's enough to have been moved by the show, which is what Bergman wants, I'm sure; but the Literature professor would have you doing collateral readings in this and comparative studies in that—readings in dream research, love research, growing-old research, dying research, and Swedish society in the postwar period research. I'm not suggesting that such studies are useless, only that they would surely render *Wild Strawberries* itself a martyr to pedagogy. The movie is the truest, kindest meditation on growing old I know of, and frankly I don't care to examine the matter any more closely than Bergman himself does, at least not while my Winnebago still has gas in its tank.

FICTION WORKSHOP One of the things you may want to try during your semester is introduce the students to the concept of grandiosity. Many undergrads don't even know what the word means, let alone grasp the concept, and one or two will assume you're referring to the Grand Canyon and such. We struggled over this for about an hour yesterday and a fine time was had by all. I kept shoving examples at them and asking them to give some back. Here's the one I offered that seemed to help them make the breakthrough:

A fundamentalist preacher I used to know showed me some lines in the Bible which indicate that at the time of the end, God will secretly recruit a small number of comparatively weak and insignificant people for special training, and these will eventually become local leaders during the reconstruction period after the second coming of Christ, when the Kingdom of God is being established here on earth. Later these same people will be sent, individually, to some of the barren planets in the far reaches of the universe, where they will create new worlds in the manner recorded in the early chapters of Genesis. The individuals will say *Let there be light* and all the rest of it, will create an Adam out of the dust of that earth, and centuries later will die for the sins of the very worlds they themselves created. (Roland Archer)

"Now *that*," said Jennifer Balle, "is a grandiose conception."

"You betcha."

"Sounds more like a science fiction plot to me," said Irate Rosenberg the Strident.

EXPOSITION I I had asked the students to bring in some examples of alliteration. Melissa Harkness showed up with a beauty from Jack Kroll's *Newsweek* review: "How comfy to be siphoned silly by the ultimate kiss of Dracula." Kroll's name comes up often in my Expo courses, along with John Simon's. I use them as examples of extremes—the positively oriented reviewer and the negatively oriented. Simon watches a show to find out what's wrong with it, Kroll to find out what's good about it. Before the semester's over we'll have an interesting discussion on why it's easier and more fun to tear something down, verbally, than to praise it. We always end up agreeing that this is deplorable and a sad comment on human nature, and afterward gleefully go back to demolishing everything in sight. I'm usually pretty hard on Simon in class, calling him the master of the sneer, but I never forget to express my admiration for his brilliance as a reviewer and the fierceness with which he defends our deteriorating language.

Kermit Waggoner was the last student I called on to read his example but I wish he had been the first, for the

115

class was a bit solemn yesterday. Kermit is a large, jovial, football-jerseyed fellow who though resembling a stunned ox in mien is one of the most intelligent writers in the group. Anyway, he rose somewhat ponderously and delivered himself of the following:

"Great green globs of gooey green gopher guts."

Relentlessly professorial despite the silly laughter, I asked Kermit from which publication his quote derived.

"*Mad* Comics."

"Ah yes."

All this about alliteration took less than ten minutes; the rest of the hour was spent trying to knock out the last remnants of the academic–bureaucratic style. Various brief exercises, and one devilish longer one: I handed out copies of a book review and asked them to extract the Specific Purpose Statement, list the main points in order, write a brief evaluation of the review, and then explain in writing the purpose of the exercise itself. This last request is useful whenever it hits you that you don't know what the hell you're doing; the students will figure it out for you, and invariably dignify your confusion with a high and noble purpose. This review (enclosed) is something I whipped up especially for the course, although only a couple of students guessed that. It has no purpose, specific or otherwise; there are no points, main or otherwise; and it's difficult to evaluate since it's very nearly devoid of content. The reviewer interprets nothing, and does so in a pretentious manner. Even though I had warned the students after the *Steppenwolf* exercise to be ready for another classroom ambush of some sort, about half of them fell into the same pit yesterday. Tomorrow I'll chew them out for it and try once again to convince them to approach the printed page

116

with a skeptical, hard-to-please attitude, no matter whose signature is at the bottom. Any piece of writing should have to prove itself to you, and I'm still surprised by the passive, almost supine, attitude of so many students who are ready to take seriously and be snowed by almost anything in print.

Wormwood and Other Hustings, by H. R. Robinette (translated by Xan Fiedler). Esoterikon Press, 229 pp., $10.95

One can learn much from a re-reading of Kafka's *Notae* in grappling with the H. R. Robinette controversy, for the new publication of the latter closely parallels the bold sorties of the former, and deliberately so—particularly in their common fascination with dramatic ambivalence. Whereas Kafka's themes never fail to illustrate the content of his work, Robinette's delightfully fussy digressions in literary conceit usually lead the unwary reader into the verdant pastureland of poetics. It is quite true that the poetry is often of a three-dimensional sort, which, though it may please the artistic palate anxious to savor esthetical tidbits, provides scant nourishment for the world-weary.

As to the actual content: only the verdict of history can pronounce the essential worth of *Wormwood and Other Hustings*. The wise critic will forbear to predict, lest license give way to presumption. The bolder critics among us (Danforth of the *Tribune*, for instance) have already committed themselves to a general letter-of-recommendation to the Muse on behalf of this author—on the basis, one gathers, of his accurate and telling references to antiquity and the sheer narrative power. It is undeniable that H. R. Robinette has an uncanny grasp of Greco-Roman culture, but the question remains: are the references always relevant to societal concerns, and furthermore, should they be? Unlike the distinguished critic of the *Tribune*, his counterpart on the *Times* couches his disapproval of the novel in metaphorical terms: Robinette, he claims, has produced a dish for the oven, which, had it been done to a turn, would have been "baked" rather than "cooked." (A jest presumably toying with the

117

inference of meatlessness, though with Broyard one can never be certain.)

As for the content of the novel itself: In *Wormwood and Other Hustings* the reader encounters one Pierre LeJuiffe, whom one easily identifies as a symbol of ambivalence and alienation, a man who earns a tentative living by grinding away (*sans* sparks) at the sharpening-stone of French academia. Specifically he is a tutor at the École Carrefour in the Fourteenth Arrondissement in the capital. The school is efficiently over-mistressed by the novel's sole female character, Julietta Parotti, a Roman transplant of some small literary accomplishment. The relationship between headmistress and tutor is, among other things, a subtle statement by the author on the prevailing hashish culture among Arab-speaking students (the Carrefour students are mainly Algerian). The central image and symbol of the novel is, in fact, a student named Ben-Barka, who combines "a veritable decadence of heterosexuality" with an obsessive desire to addictify his tutor. In the brilliant middle section of the novel, the author, employing a well-worn but serviceable literary conceit (the back-to-nature exile seeking not only self-awareness but sexual identity) wins over the reader by a stunning series of insights into human nature that manage to amuse as well as illuminate.

Though it requires the closest reading, *Wormwood and Other Hustings* is most certainly worth the effort, as the symbols sort themselves out with perfect clarity one by one; and by the time Pierre LeJuiffe convinces Headmistress Parotti that the exploration of the intellect is more sensually rewarding than any orgasmic experiments she might devise, the reader finds himself faced with a terrible question: does the primal scream of instinct rule the intellect of man? H. R. Robinette would have us believe that it does.

—Charles C. Sullivan
Literature Quarterly,
August, 1978

Wednesday, November 1

I finally wrote a letter to the *Tartan*. Funny how sometimes you don't know what you think until you start writing it down. I'll send you a clipping, assuming it gets into print.

EXPOSITION 1 Simple Simon stuff. I asked the students to figure out what's wrong with the following:

Dear Abby: I know that you receive hundreds of letters and that many of them aren't worth a reply. I don't want to cause you to waste your time, but I do hope that my letter will interest you enough to answer, for I really need some advice . . .

Not even Melissa Harkness could find anything wrong with it. I pointed out that both sentences were unnecessary, *whatever* was to follow; that they're weasel-wordy, apologetic warm-up sentences. "The letter writer should start right in with his complaint," I said.

"Or her complaint," said Melissa.

"Or her complaint."

—Then I read aloud the opening paragraphs from several of their own papers, demonstrating their habit of starting with an unnecessary bundle of deadwood. The students appeared to take the correction to heart, but many will begin their next assignment with a warm-up paragraph anyway out of habit—having understood the principle but not having absorbed it. My point is that you'll often need to

119

give them more than one exercise for the same principle.

I also asked them to write some 2 + 2 = 4 sentences that include a non sequitur and an omnibus word ("Water is a liquid; I think water is great, and it is green.") I doubt that any other instructor had ever asked them deliberately to write badly, and they went to work with an air of mis-chievous excitement.

More than anything except weak content, undergrad nonfiction is flawed by unnecessary statements of the obvious, by sweeping generalities, by preference for the abstract over the concrete and the general over the specific, by poor logic. You would do well to begin preparing exercises that will help them work out these particular crippling kinks. Merely telling them about their bad habits isn't going to do the job.

—And keep it simple, Curly. Keep everything simple. Be willing to have the students accuse you of being too simple rather than not simple enough.

FICTION WORKSHOP Dinah Bernstein's story was in such good shape there wasn't much to say about it. Unless your students are all hopelessly untalented you'll occasionally have meetings during which there's little to say about the story up for discussion. It's a good idea to have an exercise ready to whip out of your briefcase or something to read aloud. Yesterday I brought in a few bits and pieces illustrating certain principles we've been discussing lately. I read them the opening chapter of Kerouac's *Big Sur* to demonstrate how a writer's attitude toward the world combined with a unique tone of voice can carry a piece of writing, even when the piece itself is sloppily written and verging on the amateurish. I was delighted to find that the students agreed with me that it's a wonderful piece of writing.

The workshop students are required to turn in three separate, self-contained stories in all, the last one due by November 22. It's important that you give them a formal deadline and tell them you won't accept anything after that; otherwise you'll have a pile of stuff dumped on your desk during the last week of classes, by which time it'll be too late to workshop them. This means you'll have to spend the first part of Christmas vacation reading the stories, writing evaluations, and sending them by mail.

Yesterday, sensing that the students dreaded the prospect of having to write a third story, I decided to change the final requirement:

An opening scene in a novel or play. It can be a complete chapter or act, or just the opening scene. There must be at least two intelligent characters, different from each other in attitude and behavior. The scene must depict a psychologically tense situation. (A realistic situation. Not bizarre. Not melodramatic.) The scene shouldn't be static at any point, but should develop continually. There should be at least one complication in the scene. The scene should have an ending, rather than simply come to a stop—and should be such that the reader will want to read more.

As I had expected, some of the students objected to these arbitrary requirements, which they felt were restrictive in an inspiration-dampening way, and I explained—with many examples—that the opening scene in most orthodox plays and novels and films happens to fulfill those requirements. (My workshop, as I often have to remind students, is a course in conventional-traditional fiction, the

goal being to teach them the basic principles of characterization, orchestration, plotting, setting, and theme before
they go out on their own and try to imitate the work of
Robbe-Grillet, before they commit themselves to proving
that the pen itself is mightier than the word.) One of the
examples I read aloud was the opening scene from *Come
Back, Little Sheba*, to show them how skillfully and
movingly Inge uses symbols (Lola's grief over the loss of her
pet symbolizing her lost youth and, more than that, her
inability to accept the loss) and establishes the momentum
for the entire play in the first four or five pages, packing in
so much foreshadowing-conflict in a natural way that the
rest of the play unwinds itself seemingly without effort.

Funny question you asked (about occupational haz-
ards). I can't think of any serious ones offhand. The only
one that comes to mind is a sort of awkward byproduct: you
tend to talk in fifty-minute spurts whether you're addressing
students, a clerk in a drugstore, or your three-year-old
daughter. My family accommodates itself to this in various
ways: usually everybody just goes about his business,
throwing an occasional sop ("Oh, really?" or "Absolutely
right" or—when Lucy's patience wears thin—"Anything
you say, Gramps"), but sometimes I'll try to put two fifty-
minute lectures back to back and then there's trouble. Lucy
will either lead me into a closet or, if I won't go, *quite
literally* stuffs a sock in my mouth. A sure-fire measure.

Glad you liked the Henry Moore series. He seems the
sort of artist who does what he does without intellectualiz-
ing the process. He simply goes ahead, without consciously
trying to work out a new style or form; merely makes big
and little changes in the piece he's sculpting until it's the
way he wants it—but unlike so many artists nowadays he

does not then make Statements about what he has done. (My students are always ready to explain "what I was trying to do" rather than producing a piece of fiction that speaks for itself.) I have a theory that many of the best artists down through history didn't know what the hell they were doing, in a sense, but simply did it; their eyes, ears, and hands knew, but not necessarily their conscious minds. It seems to me that the more intellectually self-conscious an artist becomes the less able he is to do art. One of the reasons most everything today is second- and third-rate is that the artists approach their work academically; but a more important reason is that first-rate art, even the gloomiest, is an affirmation and we're in a time of negation right now. It's a time of such blasted morale that even the *concepts* of grandeur and nobility seem corny to undergrads.

Friday, November 3

Already getting a bit nervous about next Tuesday's issue of the *Tartan*.

EXPOSITION 1 Interesting how one class goes well and another poorly. Sometimes it's downright mysterious. It just happens that today I was more helplessly inept than in any class so far; yet the students seemed interested in everything coming out of my beard, and their questions and comments were animated and stimulating. I rambled on about interviewing, a subject that's difficult if not impossible to lecture on in a structured way: about all you can do is provide a few tips, tell a few anecdotes; and most of this is useless, since every interviewer has to work out his own methods. The basic principles of interviewing are as simple as those of good writing: Interview interesting people; get them to talk interestingly by asking interesting questions; write it all up interestingly; send it to an interested editor. The first principle can be taught, although it takes a hell of a long time for some students to understand what "interesting" means, and therefore how to identify an interesting person. The second principle is a matter of teaching them how to ask provocative questions ("looking-for-trouble questions") and is almost impossible to teach unless the student has the essential chutzpa to begin with. About the third principle I can only admit, reluctantly, that while you can't teach most students to write interestingly, you can teach them how to write less boringly—and to be intolerant of boring writing, incidentally. No mean accomplishment; it's astonishing how much boredom people will put up with.

I gave them their next assignment, due a week from today:

A five- or six-page interview with a single individual. He must be a distinctive personality who takes a definite stand and makes a series of interesting remarks on a single subject about which he's either an expert or quite knowledgeable. You, the writer, must draw some independent conclusion of your own with respect to the interviewee's stand.

These are basic requirements for any professional interview—but there were a few groans from the audience anyway. Rather than try to answer all the objections individually, I passed out copies of an interview with a local businessman, an example of a typical interview in which all the requirements are met.

Monday, November 6

I had trouble falling asleep last night, because I started to brood about the firing and suddenly wanted very much to make a fight of it. Not so much because I'm forty-seven and have five mouths to feed in a time of galloping inflation as because the firing reflects a teaching-doesn't-count attitude prevalent at colleges across the country, and someone should blow the whistle, even if it's only a tiny chirp. But I don't know *how* to make a fight of it. An hour ago I tried once again to write a formal letter of complaint to the faculty review committee, without success. I'm not even sure I have a case, at least not from the committee's point of view; they're concerned primarily with procedural matters, you see. I did manage to write a note to Professor Joe Hoffnitz, and since you asked me to keep you up to date on the political developments (your phrase), I'm enclosing the carbon.

My objection is a simple one and has to do with the collective common sense, or rather the lack of it, of the promotions and tenure committee. In blurted-out language, here it is: It seems awfully dumb for an academic department to dump a colleague who has a respectable publication record, who has served on all the appropriate committees, and who has a reputation as an effective teacher of writing, at a time when the enrollment of Writing Majors is growing while the number of Literature

125

Majors diminishes. Unfortunately this isn't the sort of complaint that can reasonably be dealt with by the faculty review committee—right?

I can understand that you may not want to involve yourself in my struggle against the running dogs of grantsmanship, but perhaps you can suggest a plausible theme for a formal complaint; or if not that, maybe you can give me the name of someone who might help me sort it all out. I frankly don't know what to do next; but I'm convinced that something should be done—not merely to satisfy my own petty need for retribution but to expose the English Department's ultimately self-damaging lack of interest in the quality of its own teaching.

EXPOSITION I The great event of the day was the wan smile aimed my way by V. Brown. Well, wan isn't quite the word; let's just say that her lip curled in a way I took to be benign. She had expected to get an *R*-for-Rotten mid-term grade but I gave her a *C*. She's doing her own work now and doing it with a little more thought. Whatever the reason for the smile, I was secretly thrilled.

I tried to compensate for last Friday's sloppiness in the Expo class by going over the local-businessman interview in detail, working in some practical suggestions that may help them in their assignment for Friday. The students were in one of their collectively stern moods, but I loosened them up with Barton's guide for asking an interviewee if he has indeed killed his wife.

The Casual Approach: "Do you happen to have murdered your wife?"

The Everybody Approach: "As you know, many people have been killing their wives these days; do you happen to have killed yours?"

The Other People Approach: "(a) Do you know any

126

people who have murdered their wives? (b) How's about yourself?"

Since this fell under the theme How to Ask Embarrassing Questions, and was therefore organic, I could pretend not to be trying to be funny. Always remember to keep a straight face whenever you think you are being funny; that way, if it turns out that you are not being funny you can pretend you were serious. Today the students laughed, so it was clear which I was being.

Then a mini-lecture on anecdotes, designed to convince them that the most effective way to get almost anything across is by means of these "little stories." An example that seemed to startle some of them was Christ's parables. Stated in abstract or general terms the principles He taught are less interesting by far than when He shows them in action by means of anecdote.

FICTION WORKSHOP The discussion of Jennifer Balle's story was as painful as any workshop discussion I can recall. The story was so hopelessly bad that none of us could come up with any Pauline compliments to balance off the negatives. Everyone in the room, including Jennifer herself, realized that the piece was worthless and there was really nothing to say. And yet we all knew that the (anonymous) writer had struggled hard and earnestly over it, that it was written by someone who wanted very much to be a writer but wasn't. What made it particularly difficult for me (emotionally) was that Jennifer is unusually poised and dignified and mature for a junior and in a way has more face to save than any of the other untalenteds. Showing her the truth of the matter seemed a terribly solemn business, and I did everything I could to cop out. You might think it would be more merciful to be merciless at such times—to tell her bluntly that as far as fiction writing is concerned she hasn't got what it takes; but I believe the dreamer should be allowed to dream as long as he can. My colleagues would deplore such an attitude and maybe you will too; but I've learned that in this matter, as in every other, readiness is all. Only once has a student asked me point-blank whether I thought he had the talent that would justify his continuing in the writing program. It would make a neat story if I could say that he was ready to hear the truth; but he ignored my "truth."

My attitude of letting the dreamer dream (hope being not exactly everything but sometimes awfully damn close to it) is probably indefensible. We are, after all, supposed to be training students in such a way that they'll somehow be professional as soon as we let them go. That at least is the game they talk around here, and such heavyweight colleagues as Luther Yerkes seem to have the illusion that when a creative writing major receives his degree on Graduation Day it means nothing less than that he's fully prepared to step instantly into print and get paid for it—in the same manner that a graduate of the Carnegie Institute of Technology (the original college of the university) is ready to march straight over to Gulf Oil or Westinghouse or U.S. Steel and take his place among the wage earners. Those of us who profess to teach fiction writing have to skirt this delicate and potentially embarrassing issue whenever it's raised, as it occasionally is. The brute fact is that only about one in twenty of our students has enough talent, will, luck, ego, and craziness to break into print on his own more than once or twice and get paid more than a pittance for it—and that certainly not at the age of twenty-one.

Ideally, a college creative writing program should accept only those applicants who have raw talent; but of course that's impossible for many reasons, one being that talent often remains hidden behind timidity until the junior or senior year. What most of us end up doing is teaching a little bit of this and a little bit of that, much of it coming under the label Pop Psychology. We teach them, for instance, that people are more interesting and mysterious and surprising than they had previously suspected (many freshmen and sophomores believe they have human nature all figured out and there are no surprises left); and whenever an opening appears we slip in a mini-lecture about this or that—whatever we happen to know something about. Can't hurt. We surely have to do *something* to earn our pay beyond discussing their unpublishable stories. And we sure as hell aren't teaching anyone how to go out and make a living writing fiction.

The self-protective euphoria is beginning to wear away, partly due to nervousness over the letter to the *Tartan* (which will be "on the stands" tomorrow afternoon), and I'm trying now to address myself like a mature citizen to the problem of transporting ourselves and our gear to the Napa Valley, if it comes to that. You'll be pleased to hear we have a friend out there who's ready to rent us a house for about half what we're paying here. I got a look at it last summer: it's up against a forested mountain, has its own water, fruit trees, plenty of room for a vegetable garden. We could even raise chickens. The Robert Mondavi vineyards stretch across the valley floor beyond the house. San Francisco is only an hour or so away.

Tuesday, November 7

There was a note in my box this morning from Professor Hoffnitz. I had shown him the letter to the *Tartan* before I mailed it, but neither of us knew as yet whether it would be printed.

I wish you hadn't sent that letter.

Scary! I raced across campus to Computer Science to find out what he meant. Instead of answering directly he scoffed at my attitude of outrage over the English department's lack of interest in its own teaching. "Research is the thing here anyway," he said.

"I know, but what about the five thousand undergraduates who pay six or seven thousand bucks apiece to learn something?"

"Do they all learn nothing, then?" he teased me. "You're an expert on the quality of teaching in every department?"

"Sorry . . . But why do you wish I hadn't sent that letter?"

He couldn't seem to tell me. I had to leave two or three minutes after arriving in order not to be late for a departmental meeting that had been abruptly called. I never did get the answer.

The dean was present, to everyone's surprise, and after the chairman had taken care of some routine matters he turned the meeting over to him. His name is Harold Atterbury—a big, handsome, well-dressed, deceptively boyish-looking fellow who, unlike many administrators I've observed, knows how to lead. Anyway, the first thing he did after being introduced was to look at *me* for a moment. Then he made the following utterly terrorizing statement:

"A rather serious and nasty situation has arisen. Irving Rappaport, the editor of the *Tartan*, has seen fit to bring some material to me which I find very disturbing indeed—material which suggests that a certain element in this department has behaved in an irresponsible and unprofessional manner. . . . And may I say that to take such internal problems to the editor of the student newspaper is a uniquely inappropriate way of doing things . . ."

In a moment it would all be out in the open, this shocking thing I had done, and twenty-six pairs of disapproving eyes would skewer me, and I would dissolve in a sizzling puddle like the Witch of the West. The same hardcharger who had faced grenade-hurling, burpgun-firing Chinese in 1953 was now having a severe case of the vapors, teetering on the edge of a kallithumping seizure of some sort that would render me incapable of communication with the outside world.

To my immense relief the dean went on to explain that a delegation of English professors had gone to see Irving Rappaport to complain about the document design program. None of this had anything to do with my letter, which hadn't appeared yet anyway.

After the meeting I raced downstairs, grabbed a copy of the *Tartan*—and ran into Jennifer Balle. I put aside my anxiety over the article to ask her how she was feeling. "About yesterday, I mean."

"I'm glad it happened," she said. "It was a good experience."

"A bit rough, though."

"I can handle it."

"You're taking it better than I am, then. It was the most painful workshop discussion I've been involved in."

"Don't feel bad about it. I've been thinking of changing my major anyway—switching from Creative Writing to Technical Writing. What do you think?"

"Might be a good move."

"I appreciated your frankness yesterday," she told me. "Don't you feel bad, now!"

"All right."

She turned and walked away with her inner bruises; but there'll be no scars, I like to think. Fortunately, she has some talent as a nonfiction writer (got a strong A in last year's Expo course). I was touched by the way she comforted me in the hallway, when it was she who needed the comforting.

Standing there in the hallway, students swirling all around me, I turned to the *Letters* section and was relieved to find mine there, unedited. I enclose a copy.

Editor: Rumors have a way of distorting the truth, as we all know, and I've heard some mighty peculiar versions of what happened when the English department's promotions and tenure committee handed down its verdict on Martin Russ.

The facts: On a scale of zero to three, four members voted zero, four members voted 1, one voted 2 and one voted 3. Translated into words this means: Lose him! (One would have thought such a lopsided tally was reserved for notorious incompetents, or at least raving Trotskyites.)

In case anyone out there is offended that I have revealed the vote in detail, let it be known that the balloting is traditionally kept secret in order to avoid embarrassing the rejected suitor himself. Professor Russ happens to be unembarrassed at the moment—although that attitude will doubtless change before this is over. The reader will understand his mood in a moment, and may even come to the conclusion that if anyone should be embarrassed it is the tenured members of the English department, who make up the committee.

Here are the reasons for the rejection, as relayed by the chairman:

1. According to the Faculty Handbook, "it would be expected that special faculty appointments should *generally* not be expected for longer than three years." (Emphasis added.)
2. The department "desires to get some turnover, and to make room for a Visiting Writer."
3. While his teaching and publication performances are considered satisfactory, Russ "has been less effective in making the administration run."

Reason No. 1 is clearly one of those technicalities which one tends to fall back on whenever there's a nasty little job to do. Interesting how the word "generally" provides a bureaucratic loophole by which a department, if it wants to, can skirt the Handbook guideline.

Reason No. 2 is equally shaky. Bringing in a Visiting Writer is a fine idea (assuming, that is, that he or she is an effective teacher, which too often is not the case); but one is entitled to wonder why the undersigned writer-teacher, who has been in place for twelve semesters, must be bumped in order to make room. There are, after all, twenty-six people in the department. (No, this is not to hint that someone else should be fired; I am in no position to pass judgment on the overall effectiveness of any colleague. There is little question, however, that some other arrangement could have been worked out.)

133

Reason No. 3, which the Chairman cited as the most telling, might turn out to be perfectly acceptable, if only I could figure out what the hell it means. The Chairman himself did not know (understandably, since he has only been here a short time), but agreed to try to find out. That was on October 3, and I haven't heard a word since. Frankly I doubt that he will be able to gather more than a peevish comment or two to the effect that Professor Russ has not been running around volunteering for committee work, nor engaged in the desperate struggle to develop fundable programs, nor even showing much interest in the problem-solving seminars that are springing up. Whatever programs I have developed have been developed in the classroom, which is where it counts (but not where grants originate, of course), and I have been foolishly content to leave all the program-developing to the other twenty-five members of the department. I have also been foolish, evidently, in thinking I could leave most of the administrating to the administrators. I hadn't realized until now that they needed so much assistance.

Somehow it's as though a tackle had been fired for not playing quarterback.

And finally I'm wondering how to square all this with a certain letter I received last year which said in part: "We feel that your performance in the areas we value . . . teaching, research, and scholarship, and *service to the Department, College and University*, indicate that your salary should be competitive with those of English faculty in a larger arena . . . This salary increase reflects our confidence in you." (Emphasis added.) There is every reason to believe that those words were written sincerely, and meant to be taken literally. One is entitled to know, then, what dreadful transgression or sin of omission has been perpetrated since that letter was written which has led to such a drastic change in attitude.

I do hope that it turns out to be something colorful, so that I will at least have that to comfort myself with—as I shuffle off, gumming my humble pie, to join the disreputable ranks of the Unemployed and Unemployable.

A final word to the instructors and assistant professors of the department. Don't squander too much time and effort on your teaching chores; the students are the only ones who pay much attention to all that. Get out there and ADMINISTRATE!

Wednesday, November 8

1:45 A.M. Can't sleep, again.

Half an insight just now after watching Wertmuller's *Seven Beauties* on Channel 13 and admiring the boldness of concept and the absolute confidence of execution—so funny, so moving, so constantly surprising. (*It is only shallow people who do not judge by appearances; the mystery of the world is the visible, not the invisible.*—Oscar Wilde. That's what I call half an insight, and the half that's right is stunningly right.) As soon as the movie ended, three little Literature professors were trotted out to perform the sort of academic analysis that has to do with brain and nothing to do with heart. I imagined harpsichord music in the background. Whenever I hear harpsichord music I load my bazooka. Basically all they said was, the film needs more work; not one of them came close to acknowledging the life-celebrating and life-mourning heartbeat of the film. And noticing an air of contempt, one for another, among those three ice-cold intellectuals, I recalled that at the departmental meeting yesterday the room positively reeked with that scent.

9:35 A.M. A beautiful day, the clock appearing to stand as still as the morning itself. The tenth birthday of Phoebe Russ. Mom momentarily heartbroken: Pheebs no

135

longer a little kid. Dad glad she has avoided getting scrunched for ten years. Phee herself presently poring over photos of Tutankhamen treasures, trying to choose one miniature reproduction from the catalogue—her reward for learning the multiplication table, having spent practically the first ten years of her life at it, with the unwanted help of relentless Fa. The pupil's attitude exactly like her tutor's about the whole wretched business of numbers: fearing and hating them passionately, finding them boring, depressing, outrageous, neither party having the least patience with the poor suckers who take them seriously. Fa following Phee around obnoxiously for a year, knowing that without numbers she'll be scrunched. Phee convinced he's the worst person in the Alleghenies.

"Six times nine?"

"I don't remember."

"Six times nine, damn it."

"Ma! He's swearing again."

From food-preparation area: "Try swearing back, Pheebs."

"Six times nine!"

"Ma—can I tell him he's a mean old bastard?"

"You'll have to ask him."

"Six times nine!"

"Fifty-four." Sweetly: "Dad, is it all right if I call you a mean old bastard?"

"No. Seven times four!"

And then, glory be, after flunking math last year, suddenly a glittering *B* on her first report card this fall, for which I deserve the Teaching Cup and she something from Tut in miniature.

A trifle shaky this morning, imagining that the

students are going to be staring at me later in the day as He Who Wrote That Letter. And also as He Who Got Fired. Getting fired does carry with it a certain suggestion of incompetence. It's not easy to play the role of Fired One in the romantic mode; accordingly, I've prepared a couple of flashy performances, veritable *tours de brute force*, for today. Curtain going up at 12:30 and again at 2:30, both shows designed to send the audience boinging up to the chairman's office with placards and bombs.

Shaky too because there may be a touch of bad-mouthing today from offended colleagues.

8:00 P.M. No action at all in No Man's Land. The usual nods in the hallway and impersonal chitchat at the coffee machine. Either the colleagues are too bloodless to be offendable, or else we have a case of total indifference. When a professional writer, intending to offend, writes a letter that fails to offend, maybe it's time to put the old Smith-Corona in cosmoline.

While we're on the subject, and pretending that you've been twisting my arm to keep you informed (instead of gently reminding me in your last letter), some of the students are organizing a protest of some sort. I know this only because an anonymous supporter slipped a copy of a guideline memo under the office door awhile back. (Enclosed.)

Letters to Dean Atterbury

1. These letters are going to be used as a basis for defense of Martin Russ. Please be clear, concise, and coherent. Don't get emotional.
2. State the reasons why you think he is an excellent professor. What does he offer to the Writing Option that is unique? Put

137

down anything that could be used by the Dean to submit to the College Council.

3. Concentrate on the long-range future of the Writing Option, and why he is indispensable to its future.

4. If you care to, state whether you prefer Martin Russ over Richard Geiren, Gretchen Wylie, or Philip Corsini. We are not out for anyone's blood, but we want to keep Martin Russ.

5. Complain about our having to choose between Martin Russ and a Visiting Writer. If this University is in the black, why not both?

6. Leave your letters in Abigail Boretsky's mailbox in the Graduate English corridor by noon, Tuesday, October 17. It will make a strong impression if we can deliver a huge pile of letters that afternoon.

7. Sit back and be prepared to wait for this process to be finished. We are not going to get immediate results.

8. Sign the petition and tell all the writing students you know about this. Our strength will come from large numbers.

EXPOSITION 1 I read aloud Kenneth Tynan's article about the meeting between Hemingway and Tennessee Williams in Havana, showing the students that because the two were so drastically dissimilar, almost anything they said or did in each other's company was interesting and revealing because of the tension arising from that dissimilarity. The article is a superb example of basic orchestration, and I recommend that you take a look at it for possible use in class. It's also useful for showing students how a writer ordinarily limits himself to a small cluster of salient characteristics and attitudes in the character he's writing about and keeps the spotlight on them throughout the article. Tynan, for instance, plays various changes on Williams as ingenuous gentleman of sensibilities and Hemingway as bumptious insensitive boor, and he stays focused on those clusters right down the line. The piece is also useful for showing how a writer can convey his opinion of the people he's writing about without getting in the way; Tynan was obviously fond of Williams and considered Hemingway a big jerk.

All this fell under the theme "writing about interesting people interestingly," but I also slipped in a few words about how to dramatically structure an interview or article. We'll be going into this more thoroughly a little later, when they're getting ready to write their two thousand-word articles.

FICTION WORKSHOP Monci Jo Nickerson dropped by half an hour before class to complain, on behalf of several members of the group, that I've been giving Ira Rosenberg too free a rein during the discussions—that I let him ramble on too long. Ira, like V. Brown in the other course, hasn't yet learned to think before he speaks. Funny thing is, the sense that he almost makes, were he ever to make it, would be useful to the class as a whole; and so I've been giving him some slack so he can get his scattered thoughts together. Judging from his writing—particularly his written critiques of other students' stories—he's not only of high intelligence but also has an unusual and interesting mind. It's just that his tongue hasn't caught up yet with his brain. That'll happen soon, probably within the year.

You'll encounter at least one Ira Rosenberg in your semester, an undergrad whose written comments are sensible and constructive but whose remarks in class are an incoherent mixture of naïveté and inanity. The trouble is, the other students tend to become resentful if not outright hostile to the Ira Rosenberg among them, mistaking his groping speculations for foolishness or put-on or sheer

139

argumentativeness; and the odd thing is, they'll begin to resent you as well after a while. I happen to like Irate Rosenberg very much, for inexplicable reasons having to do with chemistry and his furious Arafat face, and I *have* let him go too far at times. Ordinarily I keep the Ira Rosenbergs under tight control by a simple method I'll pass along in case you ever need it: simply interrupt him as he crosses the line into garrulity and pleasantly ask, "And so, what exactly is your point, Ira?" Keep doing this until it comes home to him that he shouldn't open his flap unless he has a specific point to make. Pretty soon everything he says will have a point, and in Ira's case the points will be well taken.

Ironically, he showed up today in a glowery mood and sat in silence the whole two hours. Maybe he heard about the diplomatic mission before class.

Thursday, November 9

Another departmental meeting. From 8:30 A.M. until 10:10 the members of the English faculty addressed themselves to the matter of intradepartmental communication in terms of heuristic secular hermeneutics, and succeeded in breaking new grounds of incommunicability in a most impressive manner; or, to put it another way, I wasn't sure what was going on. I do know that two motions were proposed. Of that I am certain. I also know that neither of them succeeded in moving. And if I knew what those motions consisted of, I would surely tell you. You'd probably think I was being facetious if I recommended that you learn how to say as little as possible, but well, at department meetings. I sincerely believe that most of the people in the room were doing their best to say as little as possible while seeming to say a great deal. I'll take notes at the next meeting to show you what I mean, even though it's doubtful that I can convey it secondhand: it's the sort of thing you have to hear to believe.

From the self-serving point of view, one significant event at the meeting: Professor Mildred Wilson caught my eye and sent a kindly wink across the styrofoam clutter, which I took as a sign of approval about the letter to the *Tartan*. Since she is one of only three colleagues not yet taken in the invasion of the body-snatchers, it meant a lot to me.

I used to admire Professor Saul Berliner as the most outspokenly aggressive member of the department, but lately I've come to realize that I was confusing his petulant outcries with leadership. I was fooled by his clothing (the Cattle-rustler Look), by his rugged Jedediah-bearded face, by the way his office is papered with posters and leaflets denouncing everything from the Sacco-Vanzetti injustice to the treatment of the Jonestown Nine Hundred. It took me a long time to realize that it's Professor Stanley Urbanic who is the most aggressive and down-to-earth participant in the meetings. Although his manner of speech is dry and laborious, his approach like a caricature of the pedantic professor, he usually has more to say and comes closer to actual self-commitment than anyone else in the room.

After the meeting I went over to the Science Hall of Inhumanity and introduced myself to Professor Robert Sandsmark, chairman of the faculty review committee.

141

"We deal only with procedural problems," he warned me.

"How about 'inadequate consideration'?"

"I can't say at this time."

Having just witnessed a hundred-minute exercise in noncommitment in Baker Hall, his scrupulous neutrality seemed loathsome to me.

On the way back to the office I ran into Professor Walter Kravanja, a muscular tweedy colleague with a handlebar mustache who, I'm told, gives his students their money's worth. He took me by the arm and dragged me into the nearest classroom.

"I had no part in the vote, Martin. I haven't attended a meeting of the P and T committee for a long time, and only found out what happened when I saw your letter in the *Tartan*." He said he found it bewildering that four members voted "zero" and another four voted "1." "How do you account for this, Martin?"

"I wish I could."

"You have no explanation?"

"Nothing worth mentioning. Only impressions."

"A remarkable situation."

He then offered his services "in any testimonial capacity, should they be needed."

I said I was grateful. He's the only colleague who has come forward in any way.

The phone rang as soon as I got back to the office. It was my agent, wanting to know if I'd be interested in either of two possible projects. Playboy Press is looking for someone to write a history of the Korean War, and Scribner's needs someone to ghost-write an autobiography of Mel Tillis, country and western star. I told him I was interested—and have been in a manic condition ever since. Nashville here I come. Lucy struggling to calm me down. Can't shut me up. Has run out of socks. Worried about me crashing. Told her old Marines never crash; they just crunch.

"But you *are* raving, you know . . . Are you aware that you're actually raving?" She rolled up my sleeve and pantomimed an alcohol swab and injection; but it was necessary to talk on and on, and Lucy, who doesn't believe in celebrating things that haven't happened, gave up and sat down to listen. ("Some men are attracted to women with large busts," she once remarked, "and some to women with large bums. With you it's large ears.") The suggestive power of the pantomime took effect at last and I fell asleep talking to two cats in an otherwise empty room; but on awakening a few minutes later it seemed there was a lot more raving to do, and I found her downstairs in her Gucci Treadmills (as she calls her house slippers) getting supper ready for five. Four, actually. She never eats. Probably would if she had time.

One of the network anchorpersons last year reported the results of a poll having to do with the amount of respect the public has for people in certain occupations—or rather the amount of prestige attached to these professions; and to my astonishment and delight, the occupation of Professor was tied with Doctor at the top of the list. I would've thought we belonged near the bottom, along with Policeman, Soldier, Politician. If I have to leave this business, I'll miss hearing myself called Professor—I admit that. Two years ago, after the tenure uproar, the dean and chairman wanted to take away my title and replace it with lecturer because associate professor is a tenure-track title and I had

143

just been switched to the nontenure track; but I squawked so piteously, making myself a little ridiculous in their eyes (I have enough self-confidence not to mind being ridiculous), that they let me keep it—as long as I agreed to add the word adjunct, a word I have yet to look up in the dictionary.

More on the departmental meeting this morning, now that my giddiness has subsided somewhat. I recall that we discussed the indices of humanistic concern for communication in a democratic society, as well as the structurability of psycholinguistics within the disciplines of rhetoric and cognition as an affirmation of the human spirit. A less sympathetic observer might well have concluded that the department has declared war on the English language; but what's really happening is that Doctors Ogilvy, Yerkes, Ornduff, and some of the other large loomers are anxious to broaden, if not deepen, the theoretical aspect of the department's mission, and they would have our students exploring the origins of language and the development of cognitive processes to an even greater degree. All this will be useful in teaching certain things to our students, who will then be able to go out and teach them in turn to other students—a sort of karmic-Kali pinwheel, you see, in which death keeps begetting death.

Friday, November 10

Today is the 203rd anniversary of the founding of the Marine Corps and I just received a phone call from Mr.

144

Sam Connelly, whom I've never met: all I know about him is that he is in the movie business, has never gotten over being a Marine (has anyone?), and dials my number every year on this day to pay his respects to the author of *The Last Parallel*. My wife, who takes the message if I'm out, says he's quite civilized and has a sense of humor about the whole thing. The phone call this morning reminded me indirectly of a suspicion I've been brooding churlishly about for the past couple of years—that my habit of occasionally writing about Marines has somehow been held against me by certain colleagues and was one of the contributing factors in the negative recommendation by the promotions and tenure committee last time. Of course, I've been careful never to mention Marines in class or conversation, aware of the strong student–faculty–liberal bias against the military. A colleague once asked if I planned to continue writing about Marines, and it was as if a third-rate artist was being asked if he planned to continue painting sad clowns for dentists' offices. For this colleague, and others, I suspect that my blank social silhouette has been filled in with a sort of professional ex-Marine who probably goes to sleep each night with a VFW stocking cap on his head. I have no hard evidence for this; but my refusal to sign an anti-war petition during a departmental meeting in 1973 was probably a serious mistake as far as job security goes. Although I was as unhappy about the war as anyone in the room, there was an air of presumptuousness about the thing that put me off—the presumption that we are all liberal and enlightened and outraged around this conference table, that we are naturally anti-Nixon, anti-military, anti-this and anti-that in a self-righteous self-important way that has very little to do with anything going

145

on in Washington or Southeast Asia.

(All things work together for good, however, to those who love God and are writers.)

When I got to the office I started reviewing my notes for the day's class, fretting a little because it happens to be the most boring of all Expo I classes, having to do with "empty conclusions" and "instant prose," with being concrete instead of abstract, specific instead of general; and I was dreading the prospect of V. Brown doing the Liberian Twist from 9:30 until 10:20. In the middle of all this the phone rings and it's guess-who herself, informing me she has sprained her ankle during basketball practice and can't make it to class. I hung up and said *Whoopee* out loud, feeling grateful for divine intervention. This was whispered, actually, because the walls are thin, and wasn't it Maxwell Bodenheim who pointed out that even a paranoid has enemies?

After class I was ambushed by Monci Jo Nickerson and forced into an hour-long "conference" that left me cross-eyed with exhaustion. There's nothing quite as debilitating as a long abstract conversation with an intense, intelligent, intellectual undergrad. Because I had an appointment to see another student at 11:30 there was no way to put into effect the usual evasion maneuvers. That Monci Jo is good-looking was the only comfort. When you're forty-seven they're all good-looking. Actually, it was an interesting conversation, once we got past the part about the philosophical and esthetic concerns of Literature, which is what Monci Jo said she wished to consult me about. I can say all I'm capable of saying about that inside of two minutes, but fortunately she wanted to talk, not

146

listen. With about half an hour to go she abruptly began to complain about the writing program.

"After Survey of Genres we're on our own, and I have no sense of being a writer among writers here."

"A writer can't be a writer among writers—it's a solo deal all the way."

Monci Jo began to cry.

"Whoops!"

After she wiped her eyes she explained that life is meaningless. It took awhile and of course I listened respectfully. You may be called on to deal with situations such as this—which would be bearable if it weren't that students expect you to come up with The Answer. This morning I sat like a stone, trying not to be depressed by her depression, hoping she'd give me a cue as to the category of Answer she preferred; and she did.

"I don't give a damn about anything," she said.

Time for Cassette 43. Click:

"You go through a period of thinking you don't give a damn about anything. Then you realize it's only that you care a lot less than you thought you did about many things. Then you learn that what little you care about you care deeply about. And you become more or less comfortable with that . . ." Buzz-click!

I guess old number forty-three did the job, because she floated out the door in a state of samadhi.

Another visit to Professor Robert Sandsmark, only to learn that he won't decide whether or not to accept the case until he does some research into university policy regarding nontenure track appointments: "I'll have to get back to you later." I told him I didn't have much time, that I'm already looking for another job. "Before Thanksgiving," he assured me.

I ran into Dean Atterbury in the hallway outside. This fine fellow, a social scientist by training, speaks in a curiously elliptical way at times and this was one of the times. Some of what he said is to be kept confidential but I'm not sure which part. I sense that he'll be no help at all in getting the decision overturned—not this time. I tried goading him good-naturedly by quoting a statement he made in an interview in last week's *Tartan* (an ironic juxtaposition no one seems to have noticed): "There aren't enough faculty members in Writing, and that's the segment of the Department that should be kicking and screaming." Although he smiled wryly at my jibe, he maintained the noncommittal perch deans are paid for, even after I pointed out the obvious: This member of the segment is doing his best to kick and scream.

Sunday, November 12

About the Mel Tillis thing—no, I'm not counting on it, just hoping for it. Any experienced freelancer knows better than to get overexcited about a proposed assignment; most of them peter out in the preliminary stage. You have to get used to that. My first experience with this was way back in 1958, when José Ferrer summoned me to Beverly Hills; there were big plans to produce and direct the film version of *The Last Parallel*. I talked with him for three hours, went away convinced he and I were going to make

history; never heard from him again. Second experience
Life magazine planned a big-spread retrospective look at th
Korean War, using extensive quotes from my book. The
planned to fly me back to Korea (!) so I could issu
Statements and be photographed brooding over scenes o
former fear and scrunching; the project advanced so far tha
I actually saw the half-completed layout in the editor'
office; never heard from him again. The point is that fo
every film shown in theaters, every novel or nonfictior
book published, every feature article, probably ten "projects" fall by the wayside. It's all a matter of business and
competition.

Don't think this is sour grapes. Some projects come
off, and this is what makes freelancing so exciting. There
was the time I casually mentioned to Jack Reynolds, for
instance, that it might be nice to dash off a little something
about the war in Vietnam, and about fifteen minutes
later—or so it seemed—there I am tiptoeing down a jungle
trail in Quang Nam Province in total terror (and have been
careful about everything I say to Jack ever since).

—Let me give you a bit of gratuitous advice—don't
publish anything that smacks of the "popular" if you're
serious about reappointment. During my reappointmen
uproar in 1975 I was indirectly asked to justify the existenc
of a book I had just published, and it was unmistakabl
clear that the members of the promotions and tenu
committee would've felt much more comfortable abo
having me as a colleague if I had actually publish
something like *Wormwood and Other Hustings* rather th
this modest, straightforward account of a World Wa
campaign. Here's the pride-swallowing memo I fo
myself having to write to Luther Yerkes and B. T. Orn

in response to their committee concern over the quality of the book:

May I raise a friendly objection to your questions about *Line of Departure: Tarawa*? The book is of the popular-history genre, as you know, and is not aimed at an academic audience. In a sense it would be unfair to impose an academically critical framework on it. The book was aimed at a broader audience, and its inclusion in the Military Book Club schedule confirms that the aim was not far off the mark. If you'll permit me to state the obvious and blow my own horn at the same time: this inclusion is not only a formal recognition given to few books, but an honor.

What bothers me, I think, is the implication that popular writing is somehow an inappropriate arena of effort for a writing teacher. There's no question in my mind that most of my students hope some day to produce work that will be read by a general audience rather than an academic coterie.

I'm aware that academicians are more comfortable dealing with publications that are clearly literary/scholarly, but I believe that my principal asset as far as the students are concerned is that I've published in several genres of writing—only one of which is "popular-writing."

The objection wasn't all that friendly, actually—I was mad as hell at having to defend a piece of writing that was meant not merely to entertain but to memorialize a terrible and all-but-forgotten campaign. There was no response to the memo.

In teaching writing you have to be blunt, opinionated, arbitrary, and doctrinaire in order to provide the hard surface your students need to bounce themselves off. If this approach sounds too risky I can only say that the reason so many English teachers are ineffectual is that they play it safe, never revealing their own feelings or attitudes toward

150

the material they bring into the classroom. You can get away with being dogmatic by admitting cheerfully to the students that you're coming on this way in order to help them develop their own opinions and attitudes. I've always felt that an instructor whose attitudes you disagree with is probably the one who will be of most help to you—indirectly or not—because you'll be goaded into defining your own attitudes, which are the only ones that count in the long run. ("You teach by aggravation, don't you?" a sharp student named Mario Banducci once asked me.)

Monday, November 13

EXPOSITION I The students brought in their interviews and I had them evaluate one another's work by answering a lot of questions designed to elicit specific constructive-criticism responses; then sent them away to do a rewrite if one was called for.

FICTION WORKSHOP. No student stories today; instead we took apart *A Rose for Emily* and *Counterparts* and put them back together again, spending an hour on each.

Grumbling: It's necessary to repeat yourself endlessly in all writing classes; this is simply part of the deal and you have to go along. When a student asks a question that has already been fully answered in a previous class it probably means he's ready to deal with the answer now. Ira Rosenberg raised a strong objection today, which revealed that he was tuned out when we discussed the same matter a couple of weeks ago. Briefly, Ira became irate when I instructed the class to deal with Faulkner's and Joyce's tales in the same manner as they've been dealing with the student submissions—that is, with an attitude of "How can we help this writer improve his piece?" Ira was truly shocked and even offended at the presumption of it, which is a reaction I can understand. It was necessary, however, to explain the reasons behind the presumption for the second time, and this I did without impatience, for there were others besides Ira who needed convincing. Of course, we came up with hardly anything that would have helped either writer improve his story, but because of our drastic tampering, some of the students came away with a deeper understanding of the mechanics of storytelling.

It's difficult, often impossible, to convince students that they needn't regard literature as sacred text. I don't mind this supinely uncritical attitude in literature majors, but when a writing major has it I'm bothered because I know how crippling it can be.

And another thing: Many undergrads hang on tenaciously to the conviction that literature is produced spontaneously, through inspiration alone. That Malcolm Lowry needed to write eight or nine versions of *Under the Volcano* before it all came together is something most undergrads don't want to hear. I'm convinced there's no such thing as a first-rate single-draft novel. This conviction is contradicted by the testimony of countless novelists, all of whom are lying. The only genre that allows you to get away with one draft is the journal.

The journal genre is convenient since you don't have to finish anything you start, which is the way my mind tends to run. You don't even have to finish the journal; in fact, you can't. Teaching is very much like that, by the way; you arbitrarily hack out a chunk of material and start hurling it at your students, and just as they're beginning to catch it the bell rings.

Tuesday, November 14

Never turn your back on undergrads in the classroom. They laugh and point and make rude gestures. If you have to do a lot of chalking on the blackboard, arrive early and get it up there before the students arrive.

I'm operating in paranoid gear today because of a combination of happenstances.

Frank Pellegrino, our rhinestone cowboy, objected vociferously to my evaluation of his five-minute speech yesterday. Basically, I said it was devoid of content and that he'll have to give another speech on Monday.

Kermit Waggoner confronted me after class and told me with a baleful look that there'll be a response from him in today's *Tartan*. Kermit usually appears to me as a large, genial, football-jerseyed object in the back row, but at that moment he seemed like a malevolent bear. When you're in paranoid gear everything's ominous. I wish I could believe that undergrads only lack charity, as Lucy said, rather than that they're merciless. I'm writing this in the office, having walked over to the campus to wait for the paper.

It occurs to me that English majors are less likely to strike when you're vulnerable than non-English majors.

153

(Kermit is in administration and management science.) There are only two English majors in the Expo class; the rest are from economics, design, mechanical engineering, physics, electrical engineering, AMS. I recall reading a painful account of Tennessee Williams' appearance before a group of non-English majors at Yale. They gave him a very hard time because he made himself vulnerable, as he is in the habit of doing with everyone. I also recall David Madden's informal visit to Gretchen Wylie's fiction workshop last year. In a charmingly open-hearted way he read us a section from a novel-in-progress, explained some of the problems he was having with it, and invited our suggestions. To put it mildly, the students did not turn the occasion into one of charity.

I'm going into all this because I know you don't hesitate to make yourself vulnerable in the presence of anyone who cares about you or is at least interested in a nonexploitative way, and you won't be offended if I say that the undergrads won't give a damn about you personally, that it's a rare student indeed who will mesh wavelengths with you. It's not only the age difference and the natural gulf between underling and overseer; it's the slightly morbid fascination that most undergrads have with any professor. I guess all I'm trying to say is, Don't make yourself vulnerable to undergrads. The only Over-Thirty I've ever seen make himself vulnerable and get away with it is Todd Van Elder, a jockey-size, ferociously aggressive, and unashamedly arrogant writer who stormed the campus one winter day last year.

He gave an informal talk to the English majors in the afternoon and a formal reading in Skibo Ballroom that evening. I rather admired the handsome fellow's cocksure

feistiness, his dominating theatricality, his defiant vul-
garity, and proud crassness in general. The students on the
other hand—with a few exceptions—thought he was too
sure of himself for his own good, that he paraded his
confidence too brashly; and as soon as they caught their
collective breath they began to bait him, anxious to
enlighten him as to the degree of his own foolishness. Mr.
Van Elder, who has been dealing with hecklers for twenty
years, allowed about five minutes of needling before
unleashing a storm of words at the needlers—words that
were scornful, hilarious, appallingly coarse, and friendly at
the same time. He put the cap on his counterattack by
sitting down beside Dinah Bernstein, who, judging by the
expression on her face, had been more offended by his
preening-peacock behavior than anyone, and joshing her
in a manner that not only was intimate but also verged on
the obscene. Dinah somehow managed to maintain her
poise, although her face took on the color of eggplant. After
that, no one tried to cross him.

   Neither did anyone learn much about writing from
him. One rarely does when a writer Visits briefly, for these
events are more a matter of theater than anything else (Mr.
Van Elder incidentally earned two thousand dollars plus
plane fare for his spectacular performance). For the rest of
the hour the undergraduates smoldered with frustration
over their inability to articulate their overexcited repulsion-
fascination and indignation. That Van Elder happens to be
a distinguished science fiction writer whose work is recognized even by Literature professors (often appearing in
academia-aimed anthologies) seemed to impress no one.

   Another cause of hostility was that Van Elder has
nothing remotely literary about him, even when he's

talking about literature. For those students to whom literature is a romantic fantasy, an altar at which to worship, it was shocking to hear advice such as the following: "Always put your name and address on each page, so that when your manuscript gets blown all over the editor's office while you're chewing your fingernails in your roach-infested room waiting for the illiterate asshole to get around to reading it, his secretary will be able to put the fucking mess back together again." The contrast between Todd Van Elder, who comes on like a used-car salesman having a nervous breakdown, and most of the other Visiting-briefly Writers, who are usually sicklied o'er with the pale cast of thought, was evidently too much for many of the undergrads; you can still hear uppity buzzings in certain corners about him to this day. Most Visiting-briefly Writers wraith it up pretty good in their readings, you see, forcing the audience to sit through monotonous dronings about microscopic trivia: "The triptych-window, styptic-pocked with the ineluctable castings-aside of the glass-blower's artlessness, tinted with ironic bruiselike hues transcending the ineffable sedimentary jurassics of toll-forgotten juggernauts, forgiving indifferences untold—the triptych-window (ah say) opens out onto the rose garden of the lustrous-shanked Samantha who" (etc.). The Professor Irwin Corey school of writing. No use trying to explain to those students in whose craw Van Elder is still sticking that he's an artist with the heart of an adolescent, that they'd do well to preserve whatever's left of that adolescent heart in their own bosoms if they ever hope to become writers themselves.

Later in the day, at home. See the enclosed.

Editor: Well, it's happened again. Another professor got the screws put to him here at good old CMU. This time the guilty party is the English Department which in its infinite wisdom decided there hadn't been a good screw job in awhile. And oh, what a masterful job. They fired the best damned English teacher I ever had.

I have been required to take English courses all my school years, and I never liked any of them—until this semester. For the first time in my life I have begun to take pride in my writing, to write in a way that lets me communicate what I want to say. It is really the first time I have ever liked going to class; I mean, I really enjoy it. And I'm not alone. I've talked to others who feel the same way.

Who is responsible? Martin Russ. So, why did they fire such a good teacher? Beats hell out of me. I guess mainly because he didn't go all out for departmental functions. But who the hell cares! Here is a man who devotes time to his students—remember us? We're the idiots who pay $6400 to $7000 a year to attend classes here. I guess we don't count. Well, we count as far as Professor Russ is concerned.

All I can say is, Hats off to you, Professor Russ. You deserve a lot better than this damn place. Some other institution will be glad to benefit from your expertise and energies. Thumbs up, sir; I'm proud to have known you.

> Kermit Waggoner
> Sophomore,
> Administration & Management Science

You know, Curly, the thing I like most about undergrads is their charity.

EXPOSITION I A class on the importance of outlining your ideas, your points, your notions, before writing the first draft of a review or essay or article or interview or even memo. I passed out copies of an article by Jeff Greenfield called "Columbo Knows the Butler Didn't Do It," and with a little help from Barnet and Stubbs' *Practical Guide to Writing* showed the students how Greenfield might have constructed an outline before writing the piece. * I asked them to write down the Specific Purpose Statement, and then read them aloud. In each case the student was able, after a little goading here and there, to lop off several words (*Less is more* is a principle that needs to be cited frequently in writing classes) until finally we all agreed on the single underlying point Greenfield makes: *Columbo* is popular because it shows the undeserving rich being brought low by a member of the working class. Then I had them write a paragraph outline—one sentence for each of the article's twelve paragraphs. These in turns were read aloud and cut to the bone until everyone's paragraph-outline corresponded closely with the one given in Barnet and Stubbs' book:

I *Columbo* is popular.
II Its popularity is largely due to its hostility toward a social and economic elite.

* Jeff Greenfield, "Columbo Knows the Butler Didn't Do It," *New York Times*, April 22, 1973, in Sylvan Barnet and Marcia Stubbs, *Practical Guide to Writing* (Little, Brown, 1977).

III The killers are all rich and white.

IV Their lives are privileged . . . (etc.)

All this was merely another exercise designed to give them practice in cutting to the core of the matter. For homework they're to construct a formal, full-dress outline, after figuring out what the major parts of the article are and then the subordinate parts in order. Although the students reeled and staggered into the hall afterward because the assignment seemed so difficult, they had appeared to be sincerely interested in what was going on during the class period itself; and I think one reason is that I sermonized unashamedly on the importance of outlining and they recognized the truth of it. Another reason is that the article itself is lively, funny, short, and a pleasure to read. Moral: Avoid acting like a Literature professor, which you'll do if you hand out copies of anything by Hazlitt and Ruskin and such. Save these for your postgraduate students, who may appreciate them.

I can imagine myself happily teaching a course called Dogmatic Simplistics, and doing a terrific job. Graduates would be known the world over for their eloquently succinct telegrams.

Thursday, November 16

In answer to your question: Preparing for your workshop class is usually a simple matter. About all you have to do is read the upcoming two or three stories two or three times, giving yourself a few hours between readings to let the Unconscious do its work, scribbling a few notes on the things you want discussed. In the class itself, all you have to do is ask one leading question after another—so that the students say all that needs to be said (rather than *you* saying it). By gently supporting certain comments you can drive the important points home, and in between times work in your sermonettes. Perhaps I've mentioned already that you can assign five students to be ready to lead discussions on each of the basic elements of the story: character, plot, theme, setting, style (or approach or point of view).

Yesterday I read them the final paragraph from "The Dead" to illustrate how sound and rhythm can contribute as much to the effect of a passage as anything else. I was careful to explain that the effect should always be to move or stir the reader, not to impress him with your cleverness or erudition. Professor Todd Smith was teasing me last month about the "simple stylists" I use in class for models—Crane, Maugham, Hemingway, Saroyan, Thurber, the early Joyce—and recommended such as Peter Matthiessen; but in my opinion such magnificent stylistics would be wasted on most of my undergrads, who aren't ready to understand that in order to write *The Snow Leopard* you have to be Peter Matthiessen pushing fifty.

The question of moving or stirring the reader was central to the discussion yesterday. Cindy Howarth's story had to do with the death of a youngster's beloved cow and her realization that her taken-for-granted father isn't any more immortal than the cow. The students were rather hard on it, and I suspect that's because they didn't like being moved—at least not in a way that seemed sentimental to them. The story wasn't narrated in a sentimental way, though, and I was free to tell them at length that most readers expect to be moved, that the best writers *wrench* you. I even went so far as to suggest that only Literature majors and other academic folk expect to be led through a series of intellectual conundrums or koans when they read fiction; and that while one can admire this or that writer's theoretical or experimental or innovative approach, in the end the only fiction that's widely read and reread over the long historical haul are tales told and yarns spun about people having some sort of "heart trouble."

I could smell the skepticism in the room. My students understand, however, that they're in the presence of someone decidedly old-fashioned (they're familiar with my belief that civilization became irreversible on the day the wheel was invented), and they give me lots of leeway. Later on I had them write down quickly the names of their five favorite movies—"the movies that shook you most"—and as I had hoped almost all had moved them emotionally, not intellectually; furthermore, they almost all told stories about recognizable people struggling toward something they wanted. (Bud Carr's list, however, included films by Kenneth Anger and Andrew Warhol and three other gentlemen of whose works I am unaware.)

Nevertheless, many undergrads would prefer to write like Robbe-Grillet. Fortunately no one pointed out that movies aren't novels.

"How do you write dialogue?" asked Beryl Cooney.

Undergrads don't believe that dialogue is easy to write once you've figured out what your characters need to talk about, and Beryl has looked askance at me ever since I tried to tell her that magicians rarely say hocus-pocus or even abracadabra. If you're lucky enough to have a scintillating conversationalist in your family, you can listen and take notes. My four-year-old Molly, for instance, just told me that she's the most gorgeous kid in the world. "You got it backward, man," I explained. "You're the ugliest kid and I'm the prettiest professor." You have to get right down to their level to communicate effectively.

"You fat," she followed up boldly.

"Oh yeah? Well, you fatter."

"Sut up."

"I won't sut up. You fat and funny looking too."

(At this point Head Nurse intervened, suggesting that Mr. Russ might care to join the other vets in the dayroom to watch "I Love Lucy.")

Friday, November 17

If Susan Sontag can refer to a trial, a psychoanalytic session, a parliamentary debate, and a political rally each as "an unacknowledged art form," is it too farfetched to suggest that what goes on in a classroom can sometimes be that too? While I don't see how the teacher himself can be anything but a performing artist of sorts, I suspect that the event as a whole breaks through into art itself on rare occasions—a group improvisation that comes off as a one-act comedy, for instance. (I should explain that my definition of art is very broad indeed. Since you pay attention to dreams, as all writers must, I'll admit to you that I believe they often achieve the dimensions of art at the highest level—elaborate productions for an audience of one.) There have been moments in certain classes when I sensed a "breakthrough into the sublime"; I hasten to add that it's always a communal-cooperative breakthrough in which I play a minor role. Maybe all I'm talking about is simply pedagogical enlightenment—those rare moments when teaching actually takes place.

EXPOSITION 1 The Thesis-Statement Lecture. This, as you've already guessed, is yet another class centered on the principle of cutting through to the heart of the matter before you start writing. Let's say the student decides he wants to write about whales. Don't let him do it! Force him to decide first what kind of whale he's going to write about and then what, specifically, he's going to say about it. The typical freshman or sophomore will plunge directly into an aimless rambling about whales in general if you let him.

Here's a list of the requirements for the five thesis-statements they'll be turning in on Monday:
1. Each must be clear (unambiguous).
2. Each must be a complete sentence.
3. Each must contain a *single* topic plus an idea/opinion/ attitude toward that topic.
4. Each must be defendable on the basis of reason, not emotion.
5. They must not convey obvious opinions that most readers already share.

I told them that they'll probably be required to base their final assignment (a feature article) on one of their thesis-statements. Because of this requirement they will choose their topics with extreme care, and most will bring in topics they're truly interested in. This in turn means that they'll probably write about them in an interesting or at least interested way.

You can't do too much of this sort of thing in your nonfiction course (forcing students to distill).

Tuesday, November 21

Private conferences yesterday and today with Expo I students, showing them how their interviews can be edited or rewritten or at least polished. By now the students have lost many of the bad writing habits they brought to the course, and so their interview pieces are providing me with a great deal more to be encouraging about. Now that they know I care about them (as writers, only as writers) and take their work seriously, they'll work hard right up to the last day of the semester, if only to please me. If this is manipulation, let's have more of it. "Manipulate" is the latest undergrad word for the worst kind of Over-Thirty sin, having replaced "value judgment," which replaced "cop-out," which replaced "sold out." Back in 1972, when I got started in this game, more than one student asked me with a look of haughty disdain, "You're asking me to make a value judgment?" (You got it, pal.)

The last conference yesterday was with good old Kermit Waggoner. He said something that tickled me: "In class the day after my letter appeared, I was afraid you were going to pass out Xerox copies and ask, *What's the funda-*

mental flaw?" My natural sadism rarely carries me that far, I told him.

After we had discussed his interview he took the opportunity to get a few things off his chest. With a series of anecdotes he illustrated the indifference of the administration and faculty to undergrads—stories of evasion, runaround, buck passing, wild-goose chases, official rudeness. I had heard it all before and so will you if you stay in the business more than a semester. Kermit is a sophomore and there's still time left for him to carve out a useful education for himself if he's aggressive about it. I rarely give personal advice to students (who rarely ask it), but I told him that an undergrad nowadays simply has to take the bull by the horns to get his money's worth. Most students, as I've mentioned already, are utterly passive and the only ones who get *all* there is to be got are those who in effect make themselves obnoxious, dropping by your office repeatedly, buttonholing you in the hallway, forcing you to explain and elaborate and advise—insisting that you commit yourself to their education beyond what you may consider the call of duty.

FICTION WORKSHOP We spent the whole two hours discussing Hawthorne's *My Kinsman, Major Molineaux*. With a little help from Abcarian and Klotz * I showed the students how a work of literature can be approached critically in a formalist, sociological, Marxist, and psychoanalytic manner in turn. The latter approach was the most fun—although the students found the Marxian approach

* Edward Abcarian and Marvin Klotz, eds., *Literature: The Human Experience* (St. Martin's Press, 1978).

165

hilarious—and by far the most enlightening. I demonstrated how Hawthorne's tale can be interpreted as a journey into the Unconscious, and the working-out in surprising detail of the Oedipal triangle. We had a funny discussion trying to figure out how Hawthorne accomplished this without having read Freud. The students stoutly resisted the notion of the universality of the Oedipus complex, largely on the basis that it's too damned silly to be true, and I failed to convince them that Sigmund was anything other than one wild and crazy guy.

November 21, 1978

Editor: The decision has been made not to renew Martin Russ' contract. Since his teaching and publications have been judged satisfactory, few of us can understand exactly why he is being let go. The department's reasons for it are incomprehensibly vague.

Being a former student in three of Professor Russ' courses, I feel that this move personally kicks in the teeth of every student he has ever taught. After working our butts off in his classes to learn how to write well, we're essentially being told that he's not high enough in quality for the department. In all my semesters with Professor Russ, not once have I seen any of the departmental higher-ups observing his classes. This leads me to wonder about the committee which decided not to renew his contract: on what did they base their decision?

I feel reassured by Dean Atterbury's remarks in the November 7 issue of the *Tartan*. It's comforting to know that he takes personal note of the English department and feels that its strength "lies within the writing department." However it was a little disconcerting to read his statement that "There aren't enough faculty members in writing, and that's the segment of the department that should be kicking and screaming." (It was also extremely ironic to read that in the same issue in which Martin Russ' letter appeared.) Along with most of Martin Russ' students, I personally intend to kick and scream until he is reinstated.

Each time the students evaluate the faculty, he receives outstanding comments, yet these were obviously ignored by the promotions and tenure committee. The students have written letters urging that this decision be overturned, but no one seems concerned enough to reply to them. To put it bluntly, the voices of a large number of students (who pay a large amount of money) are being outrageously ignored. Apparently what the students feel doesn't make any difference.

Soon, Professor Russ, you may be packing up your books and moving out of your office. If you need a hand, just say the word; I'm sure all of your students are willing to pitch in. It's a small price to pay for what you've given us. I wish there were more people who cared, but it will be the students who will miss you the most.
Jill Jones,
English Major, Junior

I was as surprised by the enclosed letter as I was by the one from Kermit Waggoner. You never know what students think of you until they tell you—at least I never do. The first time I saw J. Jones (two years ago) she seemed such a shapeless little thing in her defeminizing sweatshirt; she was one of those undergrads who make damn sure they've removed anything that might lead to a suspicion that they are female. It became evident quite recently, however, that she decided to allow herself to be a Jill—and are we ever glad. I have a soft spot for her anyway because she's one of the hardest cases I've ever encountered. When we first met she obviously regarded me as a barnacled oldster of the most objectionable sort, born to be argued down. I stuck with her through no less than three separate courses, nearly driving her batty I think with my relentlessly bland explanations and my refusal to get irritated, assigning her innumerable rewrite assignments and working with her on the side at her frequent demand. One day she apparently decided that her writing had improved and that I had something to do with it, and I have a souvenir of that great moment. It dates from last spring, when she turned in a breakthrough rewrite—everything clear and simple and logical at last. At the bottom of the final page she had added a well-drawn cartoon showing a haggard, bedraggled student with the hollowest eyes you ever saw, holding up a sign: I SURRENDER. It ain't art but it sure is sublime.

There was also a letter in the *Tartan* from a colleague I've never met named Roscoe Weese, calling into question "the fairness and objectivity" of the firing, suggesting that "the department was badly out of touch with the facts (or was shirking the real issues) or that the real facts have not yet surfaced," and asking that "this University undertake an in-depth investigation" to determine if I've not been "misled in a serious and unfortunate fashion." I walked over to the Metallurgy Department, introduced myself, and thanked Professor Weese for going to the trouble of writing it. He explained that he had been fired at Berkeley years ago for reasons having to do with his support of Governor Reagan's policies, and that he has been "sensitive to foolish firings, or at least to firings for irrelevant reasons, ever since." A dour, grouchy, abrupt fellow in a turtleneck, a chain-smoker with a chaotic-looking office, I took to him instantly for no explainable reason—other than that I was deeply grateful to him, which is reason enough. He also said he had been involved in reappoint-or-fire situations at Carnegie-Mellon in which colleagues in his own department have been railroaded (his word). One was thrown out, he said, because of his "brash and abrasive personality" and another "for his inability to bring in outside money." He quoted himself as having once asked at a departmental meeting, "Where does it specify in the university regulations that a man can be fired because his colleagues dislike his personality?" He seemed to assume that dislike of my personality is at least one reason for my firing, and he's probably right.

Wednesday, November 22

The departmental meeting yesterday was basically a two-hour seminar on the possibility—if not the probability—of exploring the question of the proper procedure for debate at some future time. The most noteworthy moment occurred when B. T. Ornduff boldly proposed that another meeting be scheduled as soon as possible for the purpose of taking up the question of an English department's options with respect to debating the matter of discussing important matters. Professor Florian Beeler suggested that we ought to begin the process with the construction of a model, preferably a three-stage model, which can be modified in such a way as to provide a solid basis for the initial planning discussions themselves. These will in turn, he trusts, be arranged so as to overlap structurally.

I tried to take notes today, as I told you I would, but it was almost impossible. Professor Todd Smith raised a certain motion, and there followed a discussion of some length as to the meaning of his motion. Not the implications, you understand, but the meaning itself. Professor

Smith dilated strenuously but failed to provide illumination. There then followed a discussion about the meaning of motion, in the Roberts Rules of Order sense as opposed to locomotion or the overcoming of inertia, and in the end the participants concluded that the wisest course, and certainly the safest, was to delay decision on the question of whether actual motion was in order or not.

I did capture a couple of representative quotes. The chairman had passed around copies of a chart showing ten boxes, six of them empty. There were various labels to consider. BREADTH was one, DEPTH another. SYNTHESIS was there too, I believe. Following a general discussion about the meaning of the chart, the chairman said, "We are agreed, then, that the boxes are fixed. What is *not* fixed is what's going to go into the boxes."

I had to leave a little early to keep an appointment with Homer Jurgensen, but as I was heading out I heard the following:

"Shall we next discuss the matter of finding a model from another department on which to base ours?"

"May I suggest that there are a number of possible options we need to explore first. The question is: What kind of model?" (Models and computers, by the way—particularly models *by* computers—are looming larger and larger in the department. Professor Saul Berliner is currently working out a "methodology" for a computerized paper-correcting system and planning a proposal for outside funding of a pilot project. A quote from his interdepartmental memo of November 6: "What I have in mind is the use of the computer as a communicator that puts teachers and students in more precise touch with each other.")

Later meetings will follow, and surely by the end of the semester a procedure by which we can move comfortably backward will have been worked out.

EXPOSITION 1 A few students always skip the last class before Thanksgiving vacation (spring vacation too) because of travel problems, so it's a good idea to cover material that day which you don't mind half the class missing. You can give additional exercises, for example, in some principle with which they're already familiar but still need to practice. Everything we did today concerned attention to detail. I showed them sentences in which the writer had found a more interesting way of saying something not very interesting said straight. *They crept past the snoring nightwatchman* has more juice to it than *They went by the guard, who was asleep* because you can hear the snore and see them creeping. And I made a speech cautioning them about abstract nouns to show them how nouns expressing *concepts* often deaden a passage of writing. Here's one of the examples I used: *The achievement of clarity of thought has a clear dependence on the correctness of the formulation of the problem.* Here's the improved version, verbs replacing the abstract nouns: *To think clearly, you need to formulate your problem correctly.*

FICTION WORKSHOP Can a wet teabag be "crumpled"? One was so described in Cindy Howarth's story today. I leaped on the word in maniacal glee, explaining that only something dry, usually paper, can properly be described as crumpled. My purpose was to show the students that a writer has to be fussy to the point of eccentricity, since a

171

single wrong note can sometimes ruin a short piece. Every once in a while it's good to jump in like this and grab hold of some seemingly trivial detail and worry it to death in class, the long-haul idea being to convince the students that there's an important difference between almost the right word and exactly the right word.

"This is ridiculous," said Ira Rosenberg. "What does it matter if it's wet or dry? Everyone knows what it means. Crumpled is crumpled."

This gave me an opening to point out that composition is one of the very few activities in life in which one can not only try for perfection but also sometimes achieve it.

Some of the principles you teach *will* seem ludicrous to the undergrads. I was pushing another one today that a couple of students shook their heads over—about how the careful, caring writer will do his damnedest to avoid using such common verbs as "to be," "to have," "to think," "to happen," "to go," and so on; how he tries to use verbs that go beyond merely describing the action, verbs that tell a little something about the doer as well as what's being done. He shivered rather than "got cold"; he gulped his beer instead of "drank it"; he fretted over something rather than "thought about it"; he slunk away rather than "left."

V. Brown is back, on crutches, unaware that the instructor has become a celebrity martyr and all-around Good Guy in the interval. As far as Velma's concerned, I'm still Mr. Wrong. She has evidently forgotten that she once allowed herself to smile pleasantly at me; it seems as though I'm going to have to start all over again.

About being liked. In nearly seven years of this I can only recall three departmental colleagues who showed any sign of liking me. Frankly I'm surprised there were that many, since I've gone out of my way to be friendly toward no one. I've been polite and amiable, but never really friendly. I've suffered no harm at all from this (beyond getting fired on two occasions). I do feel a little sad, though, when a student continues to dislike me openly this late in the semester. Due to the nature of the course and a lack of personal charm on my part there are usually a few students disliking me during the first weeks of the semester; but by mid-term, ordinarily, I will have won them over, in the sense of getting myself liked as a teacher—which is all I care about. Most of them are better writers by mid-term and know it, and are willing to give me part of the credit. Not that I ever ask for it. The last half of the semester is the time when I usually do the heaviest teaching, especially the final two weeks, because by now the students are relaxed and receptive. And so Velma, having missed six classes and one tutorial conference, has slipped back into the September mode and glares at me as though I'm merely another official thwarter-person; and I'm feeling glum about it because there probably isn't enough time left to do the job that needs to be done.

Friday, November 24

Above all, you should encourage the undergrad fiction writer to uncover the sense of his own individuality—or, to put it on a less elevated plane, his own peculiarities. If he has the willful egotism and talent it takes

173

to be a true writer he'll need to understand as soon as possible that his way of looking at things is unlike anyone else's. It's clear to me that the undergrads of 1978 have less of a sense of self than those of 1972 even though, paradoxically, they're more "into" themselves. And their fiction isn't as good. It's becoming harder and harder to convince the student that he or she is unique, or even a distinct personality. A strange contradiction in this era of self-realization.

You may be astonished, as I was at first, to learn how little most undergrads know about themselves. If you were to ask them to write a two-page autobiographical summary you'd find that except for the names and places and dates most of them are virtually interchangeable. And so are their opinions of things outside themselves. To come out against environmental pollution or overpopulation is about as unconventional as most undergrads are willing to be.

We discussed this in a general way in the Expo class the other day and were getting nowhere until I thought of Howard Cosell. His name is used more often as a symbol of all that is asinine than that of any other public figure; everyone from Dick Cavett to Rona Barrett invokes his name to signify The Worst. Merely mentioning the name will bring on a pained smirk and a shake of the head. What an awful sportsperson. What an awful *person*. The students, listening to this summary, nodded their heads in unison, even those who didn't know who Cosell was. And then (Aiee!) I turned around and said that after years of careful observation I've decided that Cosell is the finest sports commentator going, a man who always knows what he's talking about—although there's a widespread belief to the contrary—a superb interviewer, a man whose strong and elaborate opinions are always colorfully stated. The students were groaning in a tolerant and amused way.

"You all hate Howard Cosell, then? All eighteen of you?"

"I don't," said JoAnn Croft.

"I do," said V. Brown.

"I don't *hate* him," said Frank Pellegrino.

"Ah, he's not so bad," said Kermit Waggoner.

"I think he's vulgar," said Melissa Harkness.

"What do you think?" I asked Homer Jurgensen.

"I'm afraid I don't know who he is," said Homer, turning purple.

I let myself believe the point had been made and dropped the subject.

It's exciting, though, when you see a student's self-definition come into focus. Most likely he'll begin by making odd observations: A certain singer has "a cleansing sound" (instead of merely saying he likes her). In last year's Expo course I tried for a breakthrough assignment in this regard by asking each student to write his own eulogy, assuring them that no one but me would read it. They seemed to find this a stimulating assignment, and there was a certain amount of buzzing in the hallways over it (Did you hear the latest? Professor Russ is forcing his students to write their own obituaries. Get out the net!), but on the breakthrough front it was a total flop. Every one of the papers said the same thing, basically, Wendy wasn't perfect but all in all she was a pretty good kid.

Monday, November 27

Something on Cavett the other night rang a bell. A woman who writes soap operas had some interesting things to say about the importance of creating characters in depth when planning a long-range series of segments (rather than going at it strictly from the *plot* aspect). Cavett remarked that intellectuals—as he put it—are beginning to take soap opera seriously as a form of drama, and went on to compare them with the serializations of Dickens' novels. It occurred to me that a better way to run a workshop would be to have the undergrads create characters for a soap opera and then write an opening segment. Would certainly be a more vocationally practical approach than having them write short stories in the Literary mode, since hardly anyone reads short stories anymore anyway.

It sometimes seems to me, incidentally, that literary fiction is a genre that's being maintained and preserved rather than developing of its own accord. Those who defend it—with increasing shrillness—are a rapidly diminishing band; but in spite of the desperate denials it *is* passing away, already being replaced by movies and television. In a few years about as many folks will read literary fiction as now read poetry—another moribund genre since having been taken over by the professors.

And it also strikes me I'd be better off on the staff of a vocational–technical school with a writing program, if there could ever be such a thing. I'd get a hell of a lot more teaching done, for sure.

You asked me to keep you up to date on "the revolutionary struggle," but there hasn't been much worth mentioning. The students have been muttering ominously ever since my letter was printed, but it's been a long time now and undergraduates aren't too good at organizing unless there's a disciplined cadre at the core—and as far as ideological motivation is concerned this isn't exactly an anti-imperialist effort. There has been talk about a petition, a placard-brandishing demonstration at Warner Hall, even a Sex-in; but as far as I know nothing much has happened beyond the letters a few students have written to the chairman, the dean, and the editor of the *Tartan*. Greta Nyquist told me the other day that representatives of the student activities committee had complained to the chairman of the faculty senate, only to be told that nothing can be done until the faculty review committee accepts the case. Greta wanted to know if I had heard anything from Professor Sandsmark. I could only tell her that he had promised to get back to me before Thanksgiving but hadn't.

"We're ready to testify on your behalf, Marty," she said, frowning up at me from under her sourdough-miner's hat. She's a small but mighty senior with charm she isn't even aware of, and because she's one of a handful who dare call me Marty I have a soft spot for her. Lately she has become terribly serious about all this—ironically, more serious than I. She used to grin devilishly whenever we passed each other in the hallway; nowadays we exchange solemn nods like conspirators. I went over to the führer-bunker-like Science Hall and tried to pin Professor Sandsmark down. He didn't seem embarrassed at not having kept his word, any more than Dr. Ogilvy is at not having kept his. He said that no decision had been made but that the committee is "researching" the contradictory and confused policies on reappointments.

EXPOSITION I Another exercise in outlining. Passed out copies of a Russell Baker column. Had them extract the thesis-statement, the main headings, the ideas in order. You can't do too much of this distillation stuff.

FICTION WORKSHOP In the middle of the discussion about Bud Carr's story, Abigail Boretsky asked a tough and important question: "Why is the narrator telling me all this?"

Why indeed? I got a little carried away in trying to answer. Raved on about how people are less and less willing to suspend disbelief. That verisimilitude has become more and more important in fiction. That it's easy to believe a character exists when you can actually see him walking and talking on the screen, but not so easy to believe that *Jason arrived in an agony of contrition* when all you have is a windrow of words telling you so. That one of the best ways to achieve verisimilitude is to keep feeding your reader details to look at, to hear, to smell, to touch.

"But the protagonist is revealing his character in detail," said Monci Jo Nickerson. "Not only that, but the author is revealing himself. I thought that's what you wanted."

I didn't have it in me to say that sometimes the author's character might be better off hidden. There have

178

been moments over the past few years when I wanted to say, "The reason your story stinks is because *you* stink."

One of the most inconvenient aspects of teaching writing is that you have to read the writing of those students you are purportedly teaching writing to, which occasionally turns out to be worse than the writing they wrote before you started teaching them how to write. This can be discouraging. Sometimes I tell myself that the course is a kind of shock treatment. Even though it's true that the patients sometimes come staggering out of the clinic in a blind, deaf, dumb, and mindless condition at least you can assure their parents that when all the pieces come together again their loved ones will certainly be stronger than before.

Wednesday, November 29

It's after dinner now and I'll try to write a brief summary of a meeting I had with Dean Atterbury this afternoon.

My position was: What are you going to do about this outrage?

The dean's position: Nothing is what I'm going to do.

Upshot: Nevertheless, something may be done.

Although he admitted that if he were in my position he'd "do exactly what you're doing," the dean made it plain that he wasn't going to interfere in any way. Referring to the earlier uproar in 1975, he said that the English department had been "badly exposed" at that time, that it had had "a face-saving problem," and that he was sympathetic with the present departmental attitude of not wanting to back down a second time. To do so "would set a dangerous precedent," he said. "It would open the way for various faculty members who get turned down for tenure or reappointment to come running in protest, backed by their students."

I suggested that the department was more exposed this time because of the noisier student protest. He acknowledged that he was still receiving letters complaining about my firing, but made no other comment about it. Wanting to keep the emphasis on the hell-raising potential of the students, I told him that the chairman of the student affairs committee had come to see me on Monday, hoping to collect information toward a possible investigation. The dean didn't appear to be demoralized by the news.

I then complained that Dr. Ogilvy had promised to try to find out from the members of the promotions and tenure committee precisely how I had fallen short administratively, but that I had heard nothing from him for eight weeks; nor had my letter of November 20 requesting that the reasons for my dismissal be put in writing been acknowledged. Could the dean assist me in this matter?

"The final decision hasn't been made," he explained. "The department's recommendation is being reviewed by the college council, and after that will be reviewed at the university level. In other words, the process is ongoing. You have *not* been fired; you've been recommended for nonreappointment. It will be appropriate to provide the reasons in writing only when the final decision has been made at Warner Hall."

I let this pass. Never argue during negotiations; merely

question and explain. And when you see an opening, *suggest*—but never argue. I explained that by having the reasons in writing I hoped to be able to show that there are no reasons. The dean said nothing, always a smart move at such moments. I was compelled to ask a risky question: "Do *you* know the reasons?"

"Yes, I do."

Gulp! "Can you tell me what they are?"

"Yes, I can."

He whipped out a long memorandum Dr. Ogilvy had sent him immediately after the committee made its recommendation in early October, and proceeded to read it aloud. I was relieved to hear nothing more than an expanded version of the points the chairman had passed along to me during our conversation on October 3, plus an additional comment that went something like this: "In that Professor Russ has initiated no new programs in the Creative Writing Wing of the department, a greater burden has been placed on the shoulders of his colleagues."

The dean was unable to say who had been burdened and in what manner. I told him that according to my understanding, the Creative Writing Program is in pretty good shape just the way it is and asked him why a new program was needed. A hopeless question hopelessly asked. Initiating academic programs that can attract grants from outside the university (even when such programs aren't needed) happens to be something that is expected of most university professors. This is a fact of life I've tried to ignore for the past seven years. Why? Because I consider it disgusting. Of course I didn't tell the dean this. I don't want him to know how naïve I am.

Somewhere in the conversation he pointed out that I

181

hadn't been in print since the *National Geographic* show was aired in 1976. Without passion, knowing I was wasting my breath, I objected to the yardstick of volume being applied in this case, and cited some first-rate writers who've produced relatively little by way of quantity.

I've never thought of claiming to be a credit to the department as a writer—nor even as a teacher until these *Tartan* letters started appearing every week—but it seemed this was a moment calling for extreme measures. I produced a slip of paper I had been saving for just such an opportunity, on which I had scrawled a line copied from the Faculty Handbook:

There should always be room in the University for any individual who is so outstanding in any single dimension that he or she should clearly be promoted or retained.

The dean read it, handed it back, said nothing. I asked him if he intended to maintain his policy of noninterference if the faculty review committee were to send back a recommendation that the case be reopened.

"That committee deals only with procedural irregularities," he said rather snappishly. "There have been no procedural irregularities in your case."

"They also deal with inadequate consideration, as you'll recall."

"Your case was thoroughly considered by the P and T committee."

"That's simply not true."

He stared at me with raised eyebrows. "You think the committee made a *capricious* decision?"

"Not capricious—crazy!"

The dean burst into laughter. It seemed a good sign. I

tried to explain why it seemed crazy. "The department needs more writing teachers, as you yourself are quoted as saying in the *Tartan*. Not other writing teachers, more writing teachers. And yet the department is firing someone who's doing that job satisfactorily, for reasons that can't be justified by logic. How do you account for that?"

"I don't have to account for it. It's the department's decision."

"Yes, but it's a crazy decision. Who's to account for that?"

He said nothing. At this point I had to face the fact that I had made no headway at all; on the contrary, I had lost ground, having learned that I won't even be able to obtain the reasons in writing, at least not for many weeks.

"Someday my children are going to ask why I got fired if I was supposed to be such a good teacher," I told him. "I need to have something to tell them."

He nodded sympathetically, to my surprise. I decided to push the sob stuff as far as I could.

"Isn't there any possibility of compromise—some arrangement that might be worked out so that no one comes out the loser? I don't really want to raise a stink, or have the English department's reputation called into question. I'm not interested in whether or not anyone backs down. All I want is to be able to continue teaching here a while longer. I'm not asking to be kept on for twenty years, after all. Why not *one more year*—with the understanding that at the end of it I'll fade quietly into the sunset?"

The dean cracked his knuckles, frowned thoughtfully, and allowed as how a little something might be worked out along that line. At this point I picked myself up off the floor, all but the jaw, which remained on the rug.

"Perhaps I could go to the department," he mused, "and tell them that I support the P and T committee's recommendation, and that next year will therefore be your terminal year."

"Mm-*hmph*."

"Then you'd have that extra year. We'd all pretend that you had a year of grace coming all along."

"Om mani padme HUM," I said, or something along that line.

"It's only a possibility," he warned. "I'll have to talk it over with the department."

It was time to go—quickly, before he changed his mind. "Good day, Dean Atterbury."

"It's only a possibility, you understand."

"Om!"

An hour later Lucy was trying to convince me that another year would be "a major victory."

Thursday, November 30

EXPOSITION I Yesterday I gave out the final (major) assignment: A two thousand-word feature article.

Requirements:

Must be about a specific individual dealing with a specific problem. The problem should be one not easily solved.

Your attitude toward the individual and his or her action should be clear to the reader.

184

The article should include several quotes by the individual, and at least three anecdotes illustrating the main points of the piece.

Generally speaking, the article should show the reader something beyond what is common knowledge.

Knowing that many of the students would prefer to write about a colorless individual dealing ineffectively with an uninteresting problem, I spent much of the class time trying to counteract this natural tendency by going over a list of interesting *subjects* that students from previous classes had written about: a coal-mine disaster from a survivor's point of view; Edgar Allan Poe and his child bride; city bus driving as a profession; the responsibilities of a tribal chief of Pennsylvania Indians; and many others. Then I passed out copies of an article turned in by a sophomore a couple of years ago. The springboard idea ("My father, a stymied high-school teacher, finally establishes order in the classroom by an unusual method") was a fairly simple one, and because of the dramatic way the student presented the material the piece was exceptionally entertaining, informative, and thought-provoking.

FICTION WORKSHOP The students had read the opening chapter of *Of Mice and Men* and we spent an hour going over it line by line, paying particular attention to the orchestration between Lennie and George and the foreshadowing of all the conflict to come. We'll do one chapter per class from now on (there are only six chapters). This is the best model I know of for exploring conventional plotting in detail. Using the method of foreshadowing, Steinbeck develops the tension and suspense in such a way that you have slowly rising conflict from beginning to end.

185

It's also a good model for showing students how to convey type or personality or character with a minimum of fuss. George Milton, Lennie Small, Curley, Curley's wife, Crooks, and Candy are all vividly individualized people even though Steinbeck *tells* us very little about them; instead, he *shows* them moving around, doing things, saying things, and we can see for ourselves. Undergrads usually like the book despite its tendency toward sentimentality and melodrama. It's short and can easily be read over a weekend, which is another thing they like about it. The plotting is masterful, the way he holds off the various confrontations as long as possible, creating plenty of honest suspense.

In preparing for class yesterday I resorted to *Cliff's Notes*, which lays out the basic critical stuff. Comical how careful I am about concealing this. You can imagine the effect if it got around that I keep such stuff in my desk. I even avoid carrying it in my briefcase, fearing a kal-lithump-attack in the hallway and the students finding it as they look for my nitroglycerine bottle. Despite what some people might say, I've found *Cliff's Notes* and *Study Masters* helpful at times.

Because of all the publicity, the students in both courses are watching and listening with an intensity I've never encountered until now. This doesn't please me particularly, because the paranoid in me suspects that there's incipient skepticism behind it: He's not as good as all *that*. Because of this attentiveness I'm forced to prepare very carefully and thoroughly and to try to be the "great" teacher. Afterward I come lurching home and stretch out in a perfect stupor.

I'm not used to working so hard. University professors don't ordinarily have to work very hard, in case you haven't noticed. Of course they all act put upon and complain about how little time they have to themselves, but the truth is, they don't have to work nearly as hard as most other people. Whether I'm typical or not I can't say, but I spend about twenty-five hours a week wearing the Professor Hat; this includes committee meetings, class preparation, office hours, and time in the classroom. We get twenty-one days off for Christmas vacation and nine days in the spring. Our summer vacation lasts three and a half months. No, not two and a half, *three* and a half. I've never taught more than two courses at a time, and there are several professors here who teach only one. It's too easy to become sloppy and careless in a profession like this. The only people who have a chance to judge us on a day-to-day basis are our students, who are not yet articulate and bold and mature enough to threaten us in any profitable way, even when it's clear to them that they're not getting their money's worth.

Aside from the fact that I keep getting fired at it, I think being a university professor is a wonderful job, and I'd like to stay with it awhile longer.

Wednesday night I got to brooding about the dean's refusal to help obtain the reasons in writing, and ended up passing him a rather pushy memo as soon as I got to Baker Hall yesterday morning. Enclosed, the carbon.

Dean Atterbury: For tactical reasons I'm going to assume that the possibility you raised yesterday will not come off and that I should go ahead with my campaign. Though you did point out that the reappoint-or-nonreappoint process is still going on, there's little doubt as to the final verdict at the University level unless I continue to campaign as aggressively as I can. For all I know, that process won't play itself out until it's too late for any fighting-back to matter. Moreover, the reasons for dismissal will be the same then as they were on October 3.

Assuming that you're not particularly sympathetic with this line of reasoning, I'm going to ask nevertheless if you could let me have a copy of the memorandum from Dr. Ogilvy, i.e., the one you read aloud yesterday.

He called me into his office half an hour later and made it clear that his position in the matter is less tentative than it was yesterday: He now seems to support the notion of compromise. What was "a possibility" yesterday is "a stronger possibility" today. That's not a hell of a lot of movement but it's something, and I find it very encouraging. In response to the phrase in my memo about campaigning aggressively, he asked me to "delay the mobilization of your forces" until the college council hands down its recommendation on December 6. Maybe I'm reading too much into it but the implication, it seems to me, is that the recommendation will probably be in my favor.

"They can't get *rid* of you, can they?" said Lucy in the dark last night. "They've been working at it for three years, and they just can't pry you loose."

"The departmental albatross."

"More like Kharis in *The Curse of the Pharaoh*, I'd say."

"Scrape, *thump* . . . Scrape, *thump* . . ."

Friday, December 1

EXPOSITION 1 The Query Letter Lecture today, which included the distribution of samples of letters from free-lancers to editors. Assignment for Monday: "Bring in a formal query letter which describes the feature article you intend to write." This is a sort of quality-control test or preliminary sounding, giving me a chance to look at what they have in mind before they commit themselves to the first draft. You can imagine what a blow it'd be for a student to turn in a two thousand-word article only to be told that the original idea stinks.

V. Brown handed in two late papers after class. I teased her very tentatively and she laughed. Now *that* is what I call a major victory.

Monday, December 4

EXPOSITION 1 I had the students evaluate one another's query letters according to guideline questions I handed out—the idea being to force them to examine their own plans for the final assignment, or to examine their own first drafts if they've gotten that far. Behind all this was a desire to implant in their minds the basic principles I consider the most important in nonfiction writing: That you have to know what you're going to say before you can say it. That you must go beyond merely describing what your subject or topic is—you must decide what your attitude toward it is, and further, what specifically you have to say about it that hasn't already been said. That the most efficient and interesting way to get it across is through a specific individual rather than people in general or in any abstract manner. That the writer should worry a lot about not boring the reader. That he should avoid stating the obvious whenever possible. That an idea is only an idea when it can be developed. (Love, for example, is not an idea but a concept, a subject, a topic. To say that you're going to write an essay about love doesn't tell us anything about your idea; it only tells what the topic's going to be. Undergrads have a hard time grasping once and for all the distinction between concept and idea, and would rather turn in a series of concepts than interpret those concepts by means of a series of ideas about them.)

FICTION WORKSHOP The students have turned in their final assignments (an opening chapter of a novel or an opening scene of a play) and we discussed two of them today. Judging by these, the assignment seems a good idea; both pieces have enough built-in momentum to make the reader anxious to find out what happens in Chapter Two or Scene Two.

We also took a line-by-line look at the second chapter of Steinbeck's novel and I gave a little lecture about how some novelists have something to say to the reader and some don't. I took the position that most today have nothing to say, directly, and that what they say indirectly is usually nothing more than a vague general condemnation—what fools these mortals be. Since I was feeling cockier than usual I went so far as to claim that the three gods of modern American literature didn't have a damn thing to say but simply told interesting stories about interesting people in an interesting way. I was deliberately obtuse in all this, pretending to be ignorant that most great art "says" nothing specific. As an example of the rare novelist who has something to say to the reader directly, I quoted a passage from *Of Human Bondage*:

It is an illusion that youth is happy, an illusion of those who have lost it; but the young know they are wretched, for they are full of the truthless ideals which have been instilled into them, and each time they come in contact with the real they are bruised and wounded . . .

Tuesday, December 5

The amateur's attitude: It is *I* who am doing this thing, and I'm more important than the thing I am doing. The professional's attitude: This thing I'm doing is more important than me.

Another departmental meeting, with me stunned in the corner as usual, trying to give the appearance of being strong and silent like Gary Cooper instead of incompetent and hysterical like Don Knotts. During the meeting I happened to notice that Professor Stanley Urbanic had died. This fine fellow, who has suffered two heart attacks, always sits in the remotest corner so that he can pass away as inconspicuously as possible and not cause his colleagues the inconvenience of having to witness the passing. This morning at 9:22 I saw his eyes close, his head tip backward an inch and come to rest against the wall, his mouth agape; and it occurred to me that I was probably the only one in the room with any experience in handling corpses, warm or cold. Then another thing happened that is also uncharacteristic of departmental meetings: I felt as though I were about to cry. And at the same time felt a need to protect the dead from the indignity of being gaped at by such sterile bystanders, such cool collegiate cucumbers. And at the same time I experienced a sense of awe that such a nonevent as death could bring a long life of earnest service to a sudden close, with not even time enough to give the man his gold watch.

I seriously thought the fellow had croaked.

Knowing that my fellow academics would be retrograded even more cripplingly upon finding a corpse on the premises, I sprang into action, ready to make sure there was no pulse, ready to make the phone calls and do some unashamed grieving on behalf of the department (knowing that the colleagues would be incapable of any public emotion beyond the usual impotent petulance). As I was making my way across the crowded room, Professor Urbanic, having refreshed himself with a bit of a catnap, opened his eyes, closed his mouth, and sat up alertly—and I pretended that I had been headed for the coffee machine all along.

For a long time now I've tried to find ways of helping student writers come into alliance with their Unconscious, so as to be able to take advantage of its readiness to help us out, once we've learned its peculiar dialect. Basically all I do is tell them in various ways that when a writer is working he should avoid trying too hard: that he should first stuff his head with all the relevant research material and sleep on it—giving the Ucs. time to deal with it—and then hurl it all down on paper with no regard for grammar or structure or felicity of phrase. What he ends up with is an informal and very messy raw draft, but the ingredients of the formal first draft are now down on paper after a minimum of effort. All he has to do then is fool around with it, cutting and adding and rearranging until the cement hardens. When writers talk about the agony of writing, they're usually referring to the first draft, and the reason it's agony is that they're trying too hard. For undergrads who have never rewritten anything this seems an insane theory, coming from a professor of writing. I always tell them my stock Ray Norton anecdote. Norton was a sprinter whose best time for the hundred-yard dash was 9.5. His coach thought he could do better. One day he told Norton to run the distance at four-fifths speed. He was clocked at 9.4 (and went on to compete in the Olympics). Whether true or not, this little story made a big impression on me years ago. For one thing, it cleared up a mystery from my prep school days. Every year we lost our end-of-season crew race with Pomfret, even in my Sixth Form year when our rowers were taller and heavier to a man (well, to a boy). In the film of that race you can see us straining mightily in the foreground, grimacing like Kabuki actors, while the Pomfret crew maintains its slightly slower stroke in the background with visibly less effort. The Pomfret coach obviously knew the principle; his crews beat us every time because they didn't try so hard—or to be more accurate,

193

they avoided trying *too* hard. Our homeric heavings made us sloppy, while their four-fifths effort allowed them to concentrate on the coordination of their strokes.

Such a drastic and ugly fantasy when Professor Urbanic took his nap! My Unconscious instantly turning his "death" into a symbol of the sudden and unexpected end of my teaching career, with nothing to show for it but a corpus that's about to raise a stink. What bothers me is that the Ucs. seems to assume that I really have been fired— that is, that the decision will not be reversed no matter what I try to do about it. Basically the fantasy expressed self-pity, an emotion I've yet to experience consciously in this situation. I hadn't known that my poor old monster was taking all this so hard.

Brace up, there, old Ucs. Everything's going to be all right. Hey, how's about a little smile there, Ucs.?

Wednesday, December 6

I've been up since 4:15 due to a severe headache— gone now, thanks to Darvon, hot bath, black coffee. Ucs. evidently expecting the worst. That's surprising; consciously I'm expecting to get the extra year for sure, maybe more.

Remembering that I promised to keep you informed in detail, I'm enclosing the carbon of a note to Professor Kravanja yesterday.

Walter: You graciously offered to be of assistance if I ever needed it. I need it now. The College Council is taking up my case tomorrow. In the past few days I've learned that things aren't as black as I had thought. If you have the time, I'd very much appreciate it if you could be on hand to say a word in my behalf. I won't be there myself, and I believe that your presence could be crucial. The Council meets at three o'clock in Room 246A, Baker Hall. Incidentally I'm told that the Dean has invited the students who wrote letters to be present.

As I was heading toward my office, where I am now, I ran into Professor Kravanja, who stopped to tell me he had just been up to the deanery "to inquire as to the propriety of attending the meeting." The dean wasn't in, he said, but his secretary will call him as soon as he returns. His sudden caution surprised me and, I admit, disappointed me. The man is on the verge of retirement and has nothing to lose in giving me some general backing. It looks as though his support—assuming I get it—will turn out to be tentative, which is worse than no support at all.

Greta Nyquist dropped by to wish me luck and asked if it's true that some of the colleagues are cutting me. I told her that I've noticed a certain understandable tension in some of the faces, but that no one aside from Professors Yerkes and Ornduff have refused to return my routine hallway greetings.

The council meeting is going on right now. I'll just rattle on while I'm waiting. The Fiction Workshop lasted only half an hour today: I realized after class got under way that anyone who wanted to attend the council meeting might be shy about getting up in the middle of my interminable monologue and walking out, and furthermore that such an exit would be embarrassing for all those staying behind; so I called a ten-minute coffee break to provide an opportunity for graceful departures. When I came back, ready to pick up where we left off, I was truly surprised to find a room of empty chairs. It was good there were no stragglers; I wouldn't have been able to talk anyway, at least not for a minute or two.

I just now carried out a bit of creative lurking in the hallway (scrape . . . *thump*) and discovered that the site of the deliberations has been shifted to 255A, a much bigger room. That's a good sign on two counts: First, it means that more students showed up than the dean expected; and second, I've taught almost all my courses in 255A, and the meeting taking place there seems superstitiously favorable in a farfetched sort of way—the martyred spirit hovering, anxious to know whether it must descend to Tartarus or if it can resume the flesh.

At home. The meeting lasted for nearly three hours. The students were in a surly mood afterward and I had trouble finding out exactly what happened. Terence O'Haggarty said that everyone's furious because the meeting turned out to be "a set-up." Terence and Abigail and some of the others believe that the students were invited merely so that the administration can claim they were given every opportunity to speak their piece, not because the dean or members of the council were interested in anything they had to say. *

I don't know what's going to happen next. I presume that the dean will let me know as soon as the council hands down its recommendation. Despite the students' comments in the hallway, I'm still confident of getting one more year at least. The only thing that bothers me at the moment is

*See pages 207–10 for a student's comments on the meeting.

that Professor Kravanja, according to what Terence told me, stayed only for a few minutes and said not a bloody word.

Thursday, December 7

Last night while Lucy and I were watching *The Steel Cowboy* I kept asking her to reassure me that there's no reason to feel so lousy, and she kept reminding me that back on October 3 I had nothing (the department having fired me without qualification or apology), whereas right now it looks as though I'm going to end up with a year out of nowhere. She also kept reminding me that I now have a campus-wide reputation as a teacher the students respect. She also kept reminding me that I've raised enough hell to expose the department's lack of concern for its students and the quality of the teaching they receive. She also kept reminding me that I've fought City Hall and may have won. But then during the next commercial I'd mutter again, "Tell me I've got nothing to feel so lousy about." Over and over again, like George explaining to Lennie about the rabbits and how the two of them are gonna live off the fatta the land, she would tell me that there's no reason to feel lousy.

"Then why do I feel lousy?" I finally got around to asking.

She sighed and gave it to me straight: "Because the students are still getting screwed."

"That's it."

"Because in spite of their letters and petitions and meetings, the department's attitude toward teaching hasn't changed."

I just wrote another letter to the *Tartan*:

I want to express my gratitude to all the students who stuck their necks out on my behalf, and to say that although we may have lost the war we won the battle.

Lucy looked it over and pronounced the military metaphor appropriate ("Your parting shot, as you go goose-stepping out the gate in your American Legion cap"). As with the Mel Tillis thing, which has fallen through, she is not as optimistic as I am about the extra year.

3:10 P.M. Well, it seems I'm not going to become the Howard Jarvis of undergrads after all. The dean just called to say that the vote was negative and he has decided to follow the recommendation of the council, which is to nonreappoint.

"No extra year?"

"No."

"What's the basis for your decision?"

"I've decided that the English department's desire for variety is a valid one after all."

Friday, December 8

When I asked the dean today what had happened to that strong possibility we talked about, he merely repeated what he had said on the phone.

"Variety at the expense of quality?"

"Why do you assume that your replacement will be of lesser quality?"

I had to admit it was a presumption on my part. But I told him I was surprised by his decision not to recommend the extra year, and went so far as to say that the failure of the student protest will surely weaken the credibility and reputation of the English department. The dean replied that to have given me the year would have created the impression that the administration caves in under pressure.

"It's not a question of caving in," I suggested, "but of responding to the students and their needs."

I was wasting his time and we both knew it.

The only option I have left, as far as the overall campaign is concerned, is to approach the university's ombudsman. You'll understand why I'm not going to bother when I tell you that the post is occupied by President Moore's principal assistant.

That's about it for today, except to say that it was a day of fallen faces all around. I had the painful experience of running into Jill Jones, who had not heard the news, and of being the one to tell her, and of watching as she slumped against the wall. I also ran into Walter Kravanja, who explained somewhat defensively that "the students were so eloquent at the meeting that I saw no need to say anything."

You'll want to know how I'm taking all this. I was stunned into a state of catatonia for about an hour after the dean called yesterday, but pulled out of it when I realized that it meant we'll soon be living in the Napa Valley of California. Here's a list I've kept in my wallet for several weeks; it will explain why my disappointment is over-shadowed by joy:

Much cheaper rent
A landlady who is a friend
We can grow vegetables (and learn how to preserve them)
We can have chickens there (and not eat them)
Much lower heating bills or maybe none (woodburning stove)
Less expense for winter clothes
Much finer weather
No state inspection for cars
Cleaner air
Cleaner water
A rural setting
A swimming hole nearby
Better biking country
Better running country
Scenery!
We can endure inflation more easily there
We can endure economic depression more easily there
We can endure the energy crisis more easily there
We will have family and friends nearby
Less threat from automobile traffic
A safer setting for the kids, especially school
A less corrupting environment for the kids
A less corrupting environment for Dad (no television reception)
A better diet for the family
We will be near San Francisco
We will have escaped the drab dreariness of the East
We will have a place distinctly our own

Monday, December 11

I used to wonder about the apparent humorlessness of the Creator, but then I got to know those fourteen chickens at the Campbell Ranch. Let there be the silliest-looking bird I can think of, He must have said. Something with inadequate-looking flappers that races around the Garden on disproportionately large legs, making odd auwking noises and staring at sinners with crazed indignant eyes. Yes, let there be that. And let there also be the hippo-potamus.

Lucy and I are thinking about chickens a lot now. We hadn't known how much we wanted to raise them until it turned out that we probably can. We'll also have a vegetable garden, but we've always wanted to do that. I'm sending for the Burpee catalogue, and the first thing we'll do out there is dig up some ground. And as for the chickens, I'll bet Cara or Kay or one of our other friends out there will have two or three to spare. And when my next book is published, the dust-jacket copy, instead of describing its author as currently on the faculty at East Dreadsville State Teachers College, will say that he lives with his family in the Napa Valley, where he grows vegetables, raises chickens, and putters compulsively. And the photograph, instead of showing an eye-strained weasel of a professor in a textbook-cramped office, will show a self-satisfied rustic fool with the California sun on his face and Mount St. John in the background.

But will they respect me, those chickens? Last summer's balkers were respectful enough—at least they always ran away when I appeared on the horizon. The geese did not respect me. They ran too, but not always away—and I collected more than one bruise from their pinching bills. Obviously one of the reasons God invented geese was to keep sinners from getting too dignified. When you are required to feed three Toulouse geese every evening it's impossible to remain dignified. If you ever have to feed Toulouse geese, which are enormous, remember to carry a stick—not to hit them but so you can fend off their unreasonable, unjustifiable, unfair, and totally wrong-headed attacks upon your thigh, hip, or buttock.

Wednesday, December 13

Students keep asking me how I'm taking it. Aren't I angry? Bitter? Not at all, I tell them, and some of them look at me strangely. Every so often, though, I can sense something akin to disgust rising toward the surface. Just now, for instance, my oldest daughter told me she had been wrong about something and wanted to apologize, and it popped into my mind that Phoebe at ten showed more character at that moment—for she's a stubborn and definite kid and admitting mistakes comes hard—than I've seen from anyone in the English department.

Not that I expected any official sign of regret from the department; but I am surprised, and finally appalled, that only two colleagues out of twenty-five have had the nerve or gumption or social perspective to say anything about my troubles this fall. Nor do I need sympathy or even understanding; I certainly don't—at least not from English professors. My wife supplies everything I need in that department anyway. I'm only commenting on something I find remarkable. Throughout the nine weeks that this little drama has played itself out, only Mildred Wilson and Walter Kravanja have come forward to offer any support, and poor Walter lost his nerve at the last moment.

I'm not so naïve as to be unaware of the fact that there must be a reason for this. It is not "all their fault" any more than it's "all my fault." I think I've figured it out at last: my colleagues dislike me personally. I can live with that, knowing that most of my students like me, that my wife likes me, that Strongwilla, Millstona, and Fra Lippo Lippy, three giants of childhood, like me. But why are the colleagues not liking me? They are not liking me because they sense that I am not liking them, although I've tried to hide it. And they have earned my outright disdain, finally, by judging a colleague on the emotional level, by committee, and for taking away a man's employment because he made them a little uneasy.

EXPOSITION I Tutorial conferences today. I spent more time dispensing recognition of hard work and encouraging them than anything else. Now that all this is drawing to a close, and this journal with it, I find myself in a sentimental mood, taking long hard looks at everything while I'm still a teacher. Today to my astonishment I looked at Homer Jurgensen across my desk and got a little choked up—he didn't know it, of course. A plain, glasses-wearing, overweight young man, computer-maddened like so many of the slide rulers around here, he is also absolutely sincere and earnest. He lives out in the Allegheny boondocks somewhere and commutes by bus every day. He smiles (rarely) by turning down the corners of his mouth. He's a plodder, and plodders get me every time, no matter what field they're plodding in. Homer sat there today and told me apologetically that he's unable to come up with a subject for the final assignment. A gentle, innocent person of hardly any sophistication at all. His one passion: computers. He knows Basic and Fortran and Algol, but English doesn't interest him much, although he's made an effort this semester. He's a senior. There's no damn reason why I should continue to invade his privacy by insisting that he commit himself in print for me. If he happened to be an English major I would demand it; but Homer is an electrical engineer, and even though he doesn't appear to have a thing to say about anything at the moment, and has said virtually nothing in any of his papers for the course, it's perfectly all right: His "nothing" is at least more coherently and concisely and logically "nothing" than it was back in September. That he appears to have no personality at all isn't my business either. One of these days he'll realize that he's a unique and special person, and the individuality that's latent now will be manifest then. I'm going to give him a *B* out of sentimental respect for his earnest and sincerely plodding efforts. I salute you, Homer Jurgensen, for your doggedness. May your father and mother be as proud of you as I am.

And a note I never expected was slipped under the door of my office:

204

Your being asked to leave CMU, and in a way I'm sorry for that. I know how it feels because I've been kicked out to. I wonder where your rewrite pen will go from here. Thanks for trying.

V. Brown

FICTION WORKSHOP Lecture: How to Break into Publishing, or rather how to get published. Basically all I said was: Write good and mail good, but it took an hour's monologue about agents and editors to get it across. Most of the students went away still certain that getting a good agent is the main thing.

Ira Rosenberg suggested that the shrouds of anonymity be ripped aside in our last class, so that everyone will know who wrote what. This terrified me momentarily; not only have I forgotten who wrote what, I've forgotten the stories themselves. Over the years I've developed this wonderful ability to forget everything I don't need to remember. Sometimes it gets me into trouble, though. When alumni drop in for a chat they often want to reminisce about some apparently legendary story we workshopped together. "Remember *Seeds*, Professor?"

"Ah yes, *Seeds*. Who could forget *Seeds*? A splendid effort."

A dream just now, expressing something otherwise unthinkable. I was stretched out on Luke's bed, trying to catch the occasional winter sun ray, and I fell asleep. The dream was so startling and awful that I snapped awake instantly. I dreamed I was watching some undergrads descending a stark institutional stairwell; they were trying to locate the source of an unpleasant odor. When they opened the firedoor at the bottom they saw a number of corpses in the alley outside, all anonymous and nongrotesque. Alley isn't the word, since there was no exit. Bare courtyard. I didn't have time to count the corpses, but I'd guess there were twenty-five.

I prefer to interpret this as an expression of regret over having to leave my students stranded and trapped with the dead, rather than the obvious interpretation.

Friday, December 15

To celebrate my last day of classes, Lucy presented me with a bottle of red from the Mondavi vineyards; and as we drank it at dinner we all talked about how miraculous it is that soon we'll be able to gaze out on the very vineyards every day.

I guess this is it, then. Thanks for encouraging me to write all this down, Curly. I'm really glad you asked.

Good luck.

Class dismissed!

Addenda

December 19, 1978

Editor: In last week's *Tartan* Dean Atterbury is quoted as saying in regard to Martin Russ, "There has been a full and fair discussion of this case." If by this he means simply that everyone was given ample opportunity to speak, then this statement is certainly true. But when one puts the discussion in its proper perspective, as the prelude to a decision, it becomes painfully obvious that neither the discussion nor the decision were "fair." I don't mean to insinuate that the only fair decision would have been one in Russ' favor, and I'm not concerned so much with the actual decision as I am with the faulty methodology by which it was reached. I posit that the decision was irresponsibly made.

The politics of the decision were such that Russ may succeed himself as Visiting Writer in "extenuating circumstances." Apparently angry letters, pages of signed petitions, and the presence of students at the Council meeting to attest to Russ' value to the Creative Writing Program are not sufficiently extenuating. What, then, is? Quite probably nothing.

It was generally acknowledged by the Council and students that the only viable avenue for student defense was to reiterate the quality of Russ' teaching. Yet our stand on this issue was not unknown before the meeting—Dean Atterbury received many letters which said on the printed page what we said in person. Presumably it was not expected that the students would come up with a strikingly new way of pointing out the quality of Russ' teaching that would dazzle us all. The Council knew in advance essentially what the students would say; they also must have known that a defense of his teaching would not be enough to reverse the decision.

207

I appreciated Dean Atterbury's honesty in stating that one need not be a cynic to see there was little chance of Russ' reappointment. Further, one needn't have been telepathic to discern that many of the Council members had a decision firmly planted in their minds before the start of the meeting. I did not expect all members, particularly those who felt they had valid grievances from direct involvement in the case, to change their minds on the basis of our protest. But what I *did* expect from the Council as a whole, by sheer virtue of the fact that the meeting was held for students to protest their position, was that there should have been some chance, however remote, of reversing the decision on the basis of our testimony. No circumstances that we could have mentioned would have been sufficiently extenuating. Essentially the decision was made before the meeting, and as such, neither discussion nor decision were fair.

Why was the meeting called in the first place? There is something very disheartening about endings, about being told that one has no further recourse. I believe that the session was intended to put an end to student protest, thereby saving the English Department further embarrassment.

Decision before testimony is not the only flaw I find in the methodology. In a matter as upsetting to the students as this, there are two guidelines I would have expected the Council to follow in their procedures. First: that the case would be based on clear facts. Second: that all involved would have a comprehensive knowledge of the circumstances. I believe the Council failed on both counts.

When it was agreed by all that Russ' teaching was a great strength, attention was turned toward his alleged weaknesses. We were told that his publishing record is considered to be weak. FACTS: Martin Russ has published six books and several hundred book reviews, for *Saturday Review*, *Chicago Sun-Times*, *Washington Post*, *Baltimore Sun*, *Publishers Weekly*, among others. He has written two documentaries for *National Geographic*, one of which has already been nationally televised. He has been called upon on two occasions to work for Stanley Kubrick in a writing capacity, and has at present several

208

manuscripts in preparation and another to be published soon. There is obviously no lack in terms of volume. And what about quality?

"This exceptional book," says *The New Yorker* of *Happy Hunting Ground*, "describes combat in good, plain prose and with remarkable honesty. What he gives here is a rational account of irrationality, made the more persuasive and comprehensible by his literary control."

Says Frank Slaughter of *Half Moon Haven* in the *New York Times*, "The ability to find absorbing human interest in the dark backwaters of human experience is the hallmark of an original and sensitive talent. With this book, Mr. Russ proves himself a gifted novelist."

Clearly, it is not a FACT that Russ' publication record is weak.

He was accused of shunning administrative duties. FACTS: He is involved this year in Sword Dance (student readings), *The Oakland Review*, and is on the Independent Study Committee. This consideration was pointed out at the meeting; it was stifled by a single Council comment: "These are recent innovations." The fact is, he is *now* involved in administrative activities, and the letter he published earlier in the *Tartan* told of a letter he received last year commending his "service to the Department, College and University." If there are facts to be found here, they certainly are muddled.

Publication and administration were the two areas in which he was said to falter. But how can we take these condemnations seriously, and how could the committee make them responsibly without presenting us with the facts?

As many of the Council members remained silent throughout the proceedings, it would be impossible to gauge their knowledge of the case, though there's no doubt that some do not know him directly. As Russ was given no professional representation to defend him before the Council, it would seem that direct knowledge of the instructor in question should be highly desirable, if not mandatory, in making such a decision. A Council member who spent much of the meeting with his head

209

between his arms on the table awoke from his slumbers to say that he didn't even know Russ, but knew of one student who'd had a bad experience with him (not present). It was disturbing to see so dogmatically negative an attitude taken against a colleague on such slim knowledge. And while it was evident that most of the speaking Council members were well-versed on the particulars of the case, it cannot be ignored that not all were well-prepared to make the decision. This is fair neither to Russ nor to the students.

Whether the decision not to renew Russ' contract was carelessly made or not remains to be seen; it was, in any case, carelessly justified. It seems that a set of guidelines is badly needed in order that "full and fair" discussions are indeed just that in the future. The process by which this decision was made is in no way satisfactory.   Abigail Boretsky
                                    Senior, Creative Writing Major

                                    December 19, 1978
Editor: This is in response to the editorial in the December 12 issue of the *Tartan*, which says in part that since Martin Russ "was told several years ago that his contract would expire he knew all along that his relationship with the English Department would be limited."

While it is quite true that I never expected to stay on indefinitely, I was led to believe that I would probably be reappointed in the fall of '78. The Dean would not have directed the Chairman to make sure I came up for review this fall if there had been no possibility of reappointment. ("Wanting the English Department to explicitly consider Mr. Russ as a candidate to succeed himself in his Visiting Writer slot, I asked the Department to undertake such a review and present me with a recommendation.")

Here's a bit of background, with which I hope to justify the misguided optimism I labored under during the past two years:
—In October, '76, I was informed in writing by the Chairman

that the Promotions & Tenure Committee had voted 9–0 in favor of a two-year nontenure track appointment. (The word "terminal" does not appear.)

—In late February or early March, '77, the Dean and the Chairman visited me in my office, made complimentary remarks about my overall performance, and informed me that I was to receive a substantial increase in salary.

—In March, '77, I received a letter from the Dean and the Chairman confirming the raise and complimenting me on my "performance in the areas we value—teaching, research, and scholarship, service to the Department, College and University" and further stating that "this salary increase reflects our confidence in you."

—Later that month I received a letter from the Dean congratulating me on my appointment and expressing best wishes "for a continued productive career."

—In August, '77, I received my new contract. (The word "terminal" does not appear.)

—In September, '77, the Dean informed the Chairman that during the fall of '78, I was to come up for review by the Promotions & Tenure Committee, with the possibility of succeeding myself in the post.

—In May, '78, I received another raise.

In spite of this chain of positive reinforcement, I was informed by the new Chairman on October 3, '78, that the Committee had voted (0-0-0-0, 1-1-1-1, 2, 3) to recommend nonreappointment, and by the Dean that he intended to support that recommendation.

And finally, allow me to quote a passage from *Policy on Special Faculty Appointments*: "The committe may review all special fulltime appointments that include teaching and research responsibilities and it shall review all such appointments when they continue an individual in employment beyond three years, and at intervals of three years thereafter."

It's important to me that the students who have devoted time and effort on my behalf understand that I have not been beating a

211

horse I already knew to be dead. In view of the encouraging communications cited above, I don't believe it was naïve of me to think that I would "succeed myself" at least once.

Martin Russ
English Department

CURRICULUM VITA: MARTIN RUSS

Teaching Experience	Juniata College, Writer in Residence, Fall 1971
	Penn State University (Altoona), Visiting Writer, Spring 1972
	Carnegie-Mellon University, Associate Professor of English and Drama, 1972–1974
	Carnegie-Mellon University, Associate Professor of English, 1974–

Principal Courses Taught	Freelance Writing
	Modern Novel
	Fiction Workshop
	Writing for TV and Film (documentaries)
	Critical Writing (reviews)
	Column Writing (editorials)
	Independent Studies

Departmental Assignments	Promotions and Tenure Committee, 1973–1975
	Writing Program Committee, 1974–
	Independent Study Committee, 1975–
	Library Committee, 1976–
	Various Graduate Program Committees

Professional Activities	Manuscript evaluations for Burroughs Mitchell, head editor, Charles Scribner's Sons, 1969–1971
	Public Reading, Juniata College, 1972
	Public reading, Carnegie-Mellon University, 1976
Publications (Fiction)	*Half Moon Haven*, Rinehart, 1959; André Deutsch, Ltd. (England), 1965
	War Memorial, Atheneum, 1967; Michael Joseph, Ltd. (England), 1968
	Richthofen and Brown, Award, 1971
(Nonfiction)	*The Last Parallel*, Rinehart, 1957 Book-of-the-Month Club; Signet, 1958; Wilhelm Heyne Verlag (Germany), 1963; Mayflower (England), 1963; Books on Tape, 1978
	Happy Hunting Ground, Atheneum, 1968
	Line of Departure: Tarawa, Doubleday, 1975; Military Book Club, 1975; Zebra, 1978

BOOK REVIEWS

Roughly fifty reviews for magazines and newspapers *(Saturday Review, Washington Post, Baltimore Sun, Chicago Sun-Times, National Observer.)* Over five hundred reviews for *Publishers Weekly*.

FILM DOCUMENTARIES

Three scripts for Filmrite Associates: "Chosin Breakout," "The

Illegals," and "Anatahan." (All shown on network television
and in many foreign countries.)

Two scripts for the National Geographic series *Decades of
Decision:* "Black Winter" and "King's Mountain." (Shown
on PBS.)

DRAMAS
An original script for the television series "Ben Casey," 1960.

An adaptation of *The Last Parallel* for Stanley Kubrick, 1958.
A rewrite assignment *(Lolita)* for Kubrick, 1960.

In agent's hands: *Private Parts,* a novel. (Agent: Literistic, Ltd.)

Current project: *Two Years of French in 100 Days* (with Yves
Mirandelle).

GRANTS
Falk Research Grant, 1973 and 1975.
Research Grant, Historical Division, U.S. Marines, 1976.